D1566244

UNDERSTANDING SCHIZOPHRENIA

UNDERSTANDING SCHIZOPHRENIA

A Practical Guide for Patients, Families, and Health Care Professionals

RAVINDER REDDY, MD, and
MATCHERI S. KESHAVAN, MD

 PRAEGER™

An Imprint of ABC-CLIO, LLC
Santa Barbara, California • Denver, Colorado

Library of Congress Cataloging-in-Publication Data

Reddy, Ravinder.
   Understanding schizophrenia : a practical guide for patients, families, and health care professionals / Ravinder D. Reddy, MD, and Matcheri S. Keshavan, MD.
      pages cm
   Includes bibliographical references and index.
   ISBN 978-1-4408-3150-8 (alk. paper) — ISBN 978-1-4408-3151-5 (eISBN)
1. Schizophrenia–Popular works. 2. Consumer education. I. Keshavan, Matcheri S., 1953- II. Title.
   RC514.R3858 2015
   616.89'8—dc23   2015016085

ISBN: 978-1-4408-3150-8
EISBN: 978-1-4408-3151-5

19 18 17 16 15   1 2 3 4 5

This book is also available on the World Wide Web as an eBook.
Visit www.abc-clio.com for details.

Praeger
An Imprint of ABC-CLIO, LLC

ABC-CLIO, LLC
130 Cremona Drive, P.O. Box 1911
Santa Barbara, California 93116-1911

This book is printed on acid-free paper (∞)

Manufactured in the United States of America

Contents

Preface   vii

Acknowledgments   ix

Section 1 Facing Schizophrenia

  1 Facing Schizophrenia: Quick Primer   3

Section 2 What, Who, Why?

  2 Core Clinical Features of Schizophrenia   19

  3 What Is Not Schizophrenia?   29

  4 Who Gets Schizophrenia?   36

  5 How Is Schizophrenia Diagnosed?   42

  6 What Is the Course and Prognosis of Schizophrenia?   49

Section 3 Treatment

  7 Medical Treatment of Schizophrenia   57

  8 Common Medication Side Effects   67

  9 Psychological and Rehabilitative Treatments   76

 10 Treatment Nonadherence   83

 11 Achieving Maximal Recovery   89

Section 4 Coexisting with Schizophrenia

12 Life with Schizophrenia   99

13 Assembling Your Care Team   104

14 A Manual for Caregivers   112

15 Common Problems in Facing Schizophrenia   122

16 Managing Crises   134

Section 5 Science of Schizophrenia

17 Biological Foundations of Schizophrenia   145

18 What Does the Future Hold?   158

Glossary   165

Section 6 Appendices

Appendix A. Commonly Used Antipsychotics for Schizophrenia   175

Appendix B. Very Brief History of Schizophrenia   177

Appendix C. Recommended Resources   181

Appendix D. Forms and Lists   189

Index   199

Preface

Fortunate are those who take the first steps.

PAULO COELHO, NOVELIST

This small book has been written for anyone struggling to come to grips with schizophrenia. It may be the young man who has just been told that he has schizophrenia, and needs treatment for life. Or, a mother worried about a daughter who is "changing" in ways that remind her of a cousin with schizophrenia. Or, you get a call from the psychiatric emergency service informing you, once again, that your patient was just brought in because he is off his medications.

Having schizophrenia in your life, one way or another, will transform your relationship to it. No longer will it be something that happens to others, or in a movie, or stories in the media. Schizophrenia tends to provoke fear or anxieties in those unfamiliar with it because of so much stereotyping and stigma. If now you are *facing* schizophrenia—as a patient, a parent, a sibling, or a friend—it is your obligation to learn more about it. The best revenge against schizophrenia is to meet it squarely—correct the misperceptions and do your best under potentially challenging circumstances. We want this book to help you with that process.

We do not pretend that all your concerns and questions will be answered, far from it. However, we have distilled key elements of this complex illness, and gathered them into *sections*. Each section is more or less self-contained (some repetition was unavoidable), so that you can go *directly* to the relevant section. For example, a caregiver could go directly to Section 4 to find out more about better care for someone with schizophrenia. However, we do suggest everyone read Section 1 (*Facing*

Schizophrenia) because it briefly answer questions commonly raised by patients and relatives.

We wrote this book also for anyone curious about schizophrenia, for students who desire to relate better with families, and for anyone whose business it is to dispel common myths about psychiatric disorders.

Remember that the advice and suggestions in this book are our own and do not necessarily reflect those of any professional society, medical standards, or even other clinicians. However, our combined clinical experience of over 50 years, and feedback from patients and families, permits us to feel comfortable that we're on the right track.

Acknowledgments

KT: *I want to thank you doc!*
RR: *About what?*
KT: *I can talk to you. . .*
RR: *Oh, I'm glad you can do that.*
KT: *You don't get it, doc! I can TALK. . . to anyone!*

KT was trying to thank RR for something that hadn't been quite grasped—he was being grateful for regaining his capacity to communicate. It was a lesson—never assume to know exactly what someone else takes away from one's efforts. Likewise, when we (RR and MSK) say that we're thankful to the lessons learned from our patients and their families, they may never quite understand what we're referring to. Regardless, we want to express our deepest gratitude to all the KTs who have braved schizophrenia.

Others to whom we say thank you—they will get it!

RR would like to thank Sarah Rickerd for editorial assistance, Jenny Stolte Dewes for help with illustrations, and Sue Rudisin for helpful suggestions. And loving gratitude to CR for her forbearance, yet again.

MSK would like to thank his wife, Asha Keshavan, MD, both for her unwavering support and for her editorial assistance. He would also like to thank Laura Von Hardenberg for her editorial assistance.

SECTION 1

Facing Schizophrenia

CHAPTER 1

Facing Schizophrenia: Quick Primer

The one who asks questions doesn't lose his way.

AFRICAN PROVERB

If you or a loved one has recently received a schizophrenia diagnosis, you undoubtedly have a number of questions running through your mind. Being diagnosed with any mental disorder can feel bewildering, particularly in the case of schizophrenia—a disease that is often portrayed unfairly in the modern media. It can also be challenging to find reputable sources to answer the many questions that you surely will have.

The two sections that follow—one for patients and another for families—briefly answer questions that we commonly encountered in our years of clinical practice. However, it is useful to read through this chapter whether you are a patient or a relative.

REMEMBER, YOU ARE NOT ALONE!

Though a diagnosis of schizophrenia may seem frightening, remember that you, your family, or your relatives are not alone in this challenge. Over 20 million, perhaps many more, individuals worldwide suffer from schizophrenia. In the United States alone, there are approximately 2.4 million individuals living with schizophrenia. Given so many sufferers, there are many organizations that can provide the necessary information and support (Appendix C: Recommended Resources).

We want you to be aware that you will read and hear things about schizophrenia that may be distressing to you. However, we believe that having accurate information—the good and the bad—is the best preparation for achieving recovery. If there are confusing points in this section, do not stay confused; check out the main chapters or ask for clarifications from professionals involved in your care.

QUESTIONS PATIENTS MAY ASK

I Have Been Told I Have Schizophrenia; What Does This Really Mean?

Hearing the word "schizophrenia" for the first time can provoke a variety of reactions; and since the media tend to portray the disorder as one of "craziness" and institutionalized care, it is rare that these reactions are positive ones. Schizophrenia does not mean "split personality," which is an entirely different condition. The truth is that schizophrenia is simply another psychiatric disorder, like many other brain disorders.

The benchmark used by mental health professionals to diagnose schizophrenia will be described in detail in chapter 5 (How Is Schizophrenia Diagnosed?). The following summary should give you an idea about some of the experiences a person with schizophrenia may have:

- Having thoughts about situations, people, and ideas that are *untrue* in reality, yet feel quite real; they are called *delusions*. Other people may disagree with you, and this may seem confusing. It is important to remember that when your thinking is in a delusional "loop," it may be hard to accept logical reasoning from others, but you have to try.
- There may be experiences of hearing voices of people who are not there or seeing things that no one else seems to be able to see, or even smells that do not actually exist; these are *hallucinations*. While they exist only in the mind, they feel very real at the moment, but this is just your brain playing tricks on you because of schizophrenia! Any of the sensations (hearing, sight, smell, taste, touch) can be affected.
- You may find yourself not being able to say exactly what you mean to say. People might say to you that they do not get what you're trying to say. Or you might feel like your thoughts are coming from all directions. Schizophrenia seems to cause muddled thinking, a symptom group referred to as *thought disorder*.
- Schizophrenia also appears to change the way a person's emotions are *expressed* (also called *affective disturbance*). You may experience confusing emotions, or not experience feelings that you used to in the past, or may even feel nervous and depressed. Or, surprisingly, you may find yourself laughing when telling a sad story. Others around you may notice that you appear dull, or disconnected, or uninterested.

It is worth mentioning that no two people suffering from schizophrenia are alike. Just as each person is unique, the symptoms that each person has can also be very different. Also, just because the disease disables some sufferers does *not* mean that you're also going to be the same.

Reading about these symptoms may be worrisome, but it is important to remember that schizophrenia is not the end of the line! Some people with schizophrenia will experience only one episode, with a return to normal functioning. Others may experience longer periods of illness, yet lead a satisfactory life. However, there is no specific way to predict this (more about this in chapter 6 [What Is the Course and Prognosis of Schizophrenia?]).

Are There Effective Treatments for Schizophrenia?

Treatment with *antipsychotic drugs* (APDs) is a generally effective standard medical treatment. As you work with your *care team* (psychiatrist and other clinicians) to manage your treatment, you will be prescribed a medication that has been approved for use in schizophrenia by the FDA (medications are listed in chapter 7 [Medical Treatment of Schizophrenia]). The choice of a particular APD will be based on your specific situation—your symptoms and other factors, such as coexisting medical issues.

Along with medical treatment, you will probably receive *psychological (talk) therapies*, such as individual, group, and family therapy sessions intended to help you and your loved ones adjust to life with schizophrenia. There are therapies that help you learn how to improve relationships, if it is necessary, called *social skills training*. Depending on specific concerns you may need help with—schooling, job training, job finding—there are many programs available; these treatments are called *rehabilitation* programs. The goal of all treatments is to help you get back on track with life, as quickly as possible.

Will I Be Cured?

The term "recovery" may be better than the term "cure." Even in the rest of medicine, conditions that are considered "cured," such as infections or nutritional defects, can recur if risk factors reemerge. Most conditions are *managed* (like diabetes, which is lifelong, that can be controlled with treatment). While full recovery is seen sometimes, in most cases schizophrenia is one of those conditions that can be managed; the goal of this process is as much *recovery* of functioning as can be attained. Therefore, your care team's and your focus will be to find the most effective way of managing this condition, and give you all the support you need to achieve *recovery*.

That said, just because there is no cure at the moment does not mean there won't be one found in the future. Researchers are hard at work investigating causes of schizophrenia in order to find new medical treatments. Eventually, the cause of schizophrenia will be discovered, and with it will come the knowledge needed to produce full recovery of the condition or even prevent it from occurring in the first place.

Is the Treatment for Schizophrenia Lifelong?

Not necessarily. The first set of treatments may reduce symptoms to the point that medication and other therapies can be scaled back (under medical guidance), or in some situations stopped altogether. It is also possible for some patients to continue experiencing some symptoms throughout their lifetimes, resulting in the need for ongoing treatment. Your care team will determine when it is appropriate to lower the amount of your medication. However, we cannot stress enough that *any* changes in treatment should be done under professional supervision.

Did I Do Something to Get Schizophrenia?

No, you did not. It is understandable that you want to find a "reason" to explain why you got schizophrenia, or discover what was at fault. These questions are not answerable at this time. Not enough is known about the exact causes of schizophrenia to understand what may have led to up to it. There is nothing to be gained by the "blame game." Your focus now is to help yourself, by working closely with your care team, and with those people who will stay involved with you throughout this journey.

Some researchers have suggested a possible relationship between heavy marijuana use and the development of schizophrenia, but the evidence for this notion is still being debated. In all other instances, there is nothing to suggest that patients or their upbringing contributed to the development of their schizophrenia. Patients do not "deserve" their condition!

What Can I Do to Get Better and Stay Well?

Above all, you *must stay on your medications* (unless advised otherwise by your doctor) and *avoid* street drugs and alcohol.

There may be many reasons why you may want to stop medications—treatment is not working, or feeling that you are all well, or you think you do not actually need them in the first place, or maybe you cannot afford them. You may feel ashamed of taking medications. These feelings are common. However, stopping medications without supervision is the *main reason* that patients get sick again, and sometimes worse than the first time around.

Another common reason to stop medications is because of side effect. This is a genuine concern, but do not stop or change how you take the medicine without first checking with your doctors. They can treat these side effects quickly, or change to another medicine that doesn't have the same problems.

Using street drugs or alcohol is another no-no! For many reasons, having schizophrenia seems to increase the risk of abusing street drugs or alcohol. Perhaps it helps cope with the symptoms of the illness, or because of loneliness, or it is the thing to do when you hang out. You may have other reasons. Regardless of the reasons, what is known, however, is that the abuse of alcohol and street drugs increases the odds of not following prescribed treatments and eventually causes a relapse. *Staying clean* is a big part of staying well with schizophrenia.

There are a number of other things you can do to help your recovery process:

- Go to all your appointments
- Learn stress coping skills
- Develop regular habits and routine
- Keep communicating with your family
- Find friends you are comfortable with
- Eat regularly and healthy foods
- Practice safe sex
- Reach out to your care team or people you trust when you feel insecure about anything

Finally, one of the most important steps you can take toward recovery is to *learn* about schizophrenia, preventing and managing this condition.

Are There Things That I Should Not Do Because I Have Schizophrenia?

As mentioned earlier, you should *not stop* prescribed medications without doctor's orders and *not use* drugs and alcohol.

But beyond these two specific bans, there are things you *should* pay attention to help with your recovery process, and keep out of trouble:

- Do not skip appointments
- Do not hang around negative or hostile people
- Do not ignore your self-care
- Do not talk to strangers about your private thoughts
- Do not get talked into doing anything illegal or dangerous

What Are the Chances That Someone Else in My Family Will Also Get Schizophrenia?

There is a certain amount of *risk*, but it depends on how closely they are related to you by blood, as well their age. If a relative is older than 45 years, the possibility of schizophrenia decreases a lot. For first-degree relatives (your parents, brothers, sisters, children) the risk is around 5–10%; in other words, the chance that any one of them ever gets schizophrenia is 1 out of 10 or 20. There are all kinds of risk numbers and other factors discussed in chapter 17 (Biological Foundations of Schizophrenia).

Can I Lead a Normal Life?

In many cases, yes, though it very much depends on the seriousness of your condition, which is difficult to predict in the beginning. If your symptoms are mild, or are well managed with treatment, it is possible to get a job, live independently, have friends, find a partner, and do other normal things.

If your symptoms are more severe, or if your treatment is not fully effective, the notion of "normal" may be different. Adjustments may need to be made in the way you live your life, but still find satisfaction with the way things are. You may require some amount of support with housing, money, or other aspects of life. As a society, we have moved away from institutionalized (long-term inpatient) care, preferring to offer patients skills to support independent living. Even if, for example, you are not capable of living on your own, there is plenty of help—supportive housing programs and supervised apartments—that is discussed in detail in chapter 15 (Common Problems in Facing Schizophrenia).

Beyond the Help That My Family May Provide Where Else Can I Find More Assistance?

If you need more help, a good place to start is your care team. Your psychiatrist, nurse, therapist, case worker, or social services representative should provide you with referrals to local resources, whether it is getting medical information or getting rehabilitation services (commonly called *rehab*). There are also many organizations that help patients with schizophrenia; see a list of these resources in Appendix C of this book.

Will Other People Understand What I'm Going Through?

Schizophrenia may be difficult to fully grasp for others who are not going through it themselves. You may already have had this experience—when you tell someone the way your thoughts seem to you, they do not seem to understand what you are saying. But, remember, you are not alone. Thousands of other people have similar experiences, and talking to some of them may allow some relief ("somebody else gets it!"). Also, some of your family members may be very understanding of your situation. Talk to them and you may be surprised at the amount of support you will receive from them

Of course, your care team has a lot of experience working with sufferers of schizophrenia. They will listen to you and support you in ways that are helpful. There also is group therapy, as well as social groups for patients; all of these can give you the support you're seeking. Also look for peer- and family support groups in your area such as NAMI and SARDAA (see Appendix C).

Does Having Schizophrenia Mean That I'm Stupid?

No. While some cognitive (thinking) difficulties are part of this illness, especially early in the course of the illness, they generally do not continue to get worse. There are treatments, such as *cognitive remediation* therapies, that may help improve such cognitive challenges (see chapter 9 [Psychological and Rehabilitative Treatments]).

QUESTIONS FAMILY AND FRIENDS MAY ASK

Is Schizophrenia Even a Real Condition?

Yes. Those people who claim that schizophrenia is not a real disease will quote Dr. R. D. Laing (1927–1989), who famously stated in 1967: "There is no such condition as schizophrenia, but the label is a social fact." Others have argued that schizophrenia is an invention of the psychiatric establishment. These ideas have no rationale or scientific basis. Of course, the idea of being labeled "schizophrenic" is very upsetting. However, to accept that schizophrenia is not real can have very serious consequences, such as denying appropriate treatment and even blaming the person for his or her psychosis, rather than the illness.

How Do I Know That My Loved One Has Schizophrenia?

The only way to know for sure that your loved one has schizophrenia is to have a psychiatric evaluation, which will also help rule out other conditions with similar symptoms. Family members are usually the ones to initiate this evaluation after seeing their loved ones struggle with behaviors that may indicate a psychiatric disorder. In the case of schizophrenia, these indicators may be as obvious as the presence of false beliefs or hallucinations, or as subtle as noticing a decline in your loved one's ability to form organized thoughts.

Identifying schizophrenia is complicated by the fact that quite a number of patients are unaware of their illness. Even if you suspect the condition on the basis of signs like decreased emotional responses, or increasingly odd behaviors, persuading your loved one to visit the doctor may be challenging. However, it is important to try to get that evaluation before behavior deteriorates to the point of a crisis.

Did "Bad" Parenting Cause Schizophrenia?

No. In the past there was a tendency to blame the mother for her children's condition. However, there is no scientific evidence that any particular type of parenting results in schizophrenia. However, there are certain ways of relating to each other in a family that can be unhelpful to people with schizophrenia, such as hostile communication, overprotectiveness, or excessive criticism (called high *expressed emotions*). This form of communication and its effect on treatment outcome are discussed further in chapter 16 (Managing Crises).

Did Drug Abuse Cause Schizophrenia?

The connections between drug use and schizophrenia are not entirely clear; there is no consensus on research findings linking schizophrenia and the use of marijuana, LSD, PCP, or any other street drug. What we do know is that the chronic use of mind-altering drugs can damage the parts of the brain associated with intellectual function and memory, potentially aggravating the symptoms of a person with preexisting schizophrenia, and interfering with treatment. See more about this in chapter 15 (Common Problems in Facing Schizophrenia).

How Can I Understand the Suffering of Someone with Schizophrenia?

Understanding what your loved one is going through (known as *empathy*) may be difficult, as society's portrayals of schizophrenia patients are often wildly inaccurate or unfair. However, there are resources that can help you get some insight into your loved one's condition. One is the movie *A Beautiful Mind*, which portrays the delusions and hallucinations experienced by the Nobel Prize–winning mathematician John Nash. There are also many books and websites that address the experience of schizophrenia (see list in Appendix C).

Your loved one can also give you quite a bit of insight into his or her particular experience, as long as you are able to listen without judgment. Hearing a person describe his or her delusions and hallucinations can be difficult. You may feel compelled to argue that these experiences are not real in an effort to comfort your loved one, or you may find yourself feeling dismissive of the patient's *lived reality*. If you are able to suppress the urge to react, and listen with an open mind, you will better appreciate your loved one's unique experiences.

Will I Catch Schizophrenia? What Are the Risks of Me Getting Schizophrenia?

You cannot *catch* schizophrenia; it is a brain disorder that develops in some people, due to changes in the way the brain develops and functions. Although the exact cause of schizophrenia is not yet known, it probably involves many complex brain processes (see chapter 17).

Less than one out of every 100 people has the risk of developing schizophrenia in their lifetime. If you are related to a person with schizophrenia, your risk of developing the disease increases based on the closeness of the biological relationship. However, genes are *not solely* responsible for the condition. Research findings on the risk for different groups of relatives are presented in chapter 17 (Biological Foundations of Schizophrenia).

What Is the Most Helpful Way to Communicate with a Person with Schizophrenia?

When patients are doing well and not impaired by their symptoms, communication can be normal. It is when patients are in the midst of delusions, hallucinations, or disordered thinking that having a free-flowing conversation can be difficult. At any time, though, patience, understanding, and compassion are valuable, but more so when he or she is highly symptomatic, particularly with suspiciousness or paranoid delusions.

Essential considerations when beginning a conversation:

- Be mindful of the circumstances (not too many people around)
- Choose a quiet and comfortable place

- Use simple speech, in an even or warm tone of voice
- Do not "talk down"
- Keep conversations brief, or as long as tolerated
- Pass along information in small bits at a time
- Repetitions may be necessary
- Watch for signs of increasing agitation, and terminate the conversation if this occurs

Bear in mind that successful communication may not necessarily translate into successful actions (e.g., mentioning that an appointment has been made is no guarantee that it will be kept). Such difficulties may have more to do with attention and memory problems, rather than stubbornness. It is important to remind yourself that it is schizophrenia, and *not the person*, that is behind these communication challenges.

What Can I Do to Help with the Treatment?

As the family member or friend of someone with schizophrenia, you can have a *significant impact* on treatment outcomes. That said, however, the kinds of help you are able to provide depend on the degree of your involvement, ability, and resources available to you. If it is daily help, then one of the most valuable forms of assistance is with medication reminders. Beyond that, encouraging a healthy lifestyle, regular mealtimes, good hygiene, and providing company (even if it is quiet time) are very valuable. If you are less intensively involved, there still are many meaningful ways to help: ensuring that all appointments are kept, organizing transportation, and timely medication refills.

If you are open to it, attending family or group therapy sessions with the patient can help deepen your relationship and address any concerns that may come up with caregiving. Beyond practical help, advocacy on behalf of the patient (with care teams and organizations) will further assure your loved one receives the treatment he or she needs.

On the other hand, one has to be careful that caregiving efforts do not create *learned helplessness*. Treating the patient in a child-like manner and overprotection can lead a conditioning process in which the patient begins to feel incapable of taking care of himself or herself, and consequently becomes complacent and dependent on caregivers. Once this helplessness is established, it is a difficult process to reverse.

Will Schizophrenia Lead to Violent Behavior?

Not necessarily. On average, the tendency toward violent behaviors among persons with schizophrenia is no greater than in the general population at large. While there are some patients who do act aggressively, often the result of paranoia or other delusions, these symptoms of schizophrenia can be controlled or lessened with treatment. In chapter 16 (Managing Crises) we discuss more on a variety of crises, including violence.

What Kind of Crises Can Happen?

Although many patients can have long periods of stability with optimal treatment, there also can be periods of waxing and waning symptom severity. For a wide variety of reasons (e.g., stress, stopping medicines) the potential for crisis always exists. Learning to recognize the signs of worsening (chapter 16 [Managing Crises]) will go a long way to reducing the risk of full-blown crises because timely interventions can be initiated. However, not all crises are major, and do not require high-level interventions. Some judgment on your part is required to assess the situation, but it is generally better to err on the side of caution.

Extreme crises that require an emergency response (*call 9-1-1*) include suicidal or violent behaviors, or other dangerous behaviors (e.g., lighting fires). Fortunately, these are rare *when* patients are in active treatment. Severe crises are more likely with treatment nonadherence (stopping medicine and other care), and very rarely emerge out of the blue. Typically there is a gradual worsening of symptoms and behaviors before the point of crises. Therefore, at the earliest signs of trouble (with time, you will get better at identifying these signs), steps should be taken—alerting the care team is the first step; alternatively contacting a *crisis center* (make sure you have contact information handy). These professionals will guide you through the crisis. As Benjamin Franklin wisely said, an ounce of prevention is better than a pound of cure!

A valuable skill for caregivers is to know how to *defuse* a difficult situation, also referred to as *de-escalation*. More than a specific method, it is really about empathy, attitude, common sense, and good observation (chapter 16 [Managing Crises]).

How Can We Minimize the Risk of Crises?

You will hear this often: ensure that the patient is taking medications as prescribed and keeping up with follow-up appointments. Stopping medication, whether due to the cost of medication, or the mistaken belief that the patient has been "cured," is the main reason for relapse and crisis. However, highly stressful situations or ongoing stresses (that can't be resolved) also increase the risk of relapse. For example, being thrust into unfamiliar circumstances can be disorienting, and increase stress. In time you will learn what situations, unique to your loved one, are stressful.

In addition to treatment adherence, you can help your loved one develop healthy routines and habits at home, encourage fresh air and exercise, and promote a healthy diet. These healthful practices create a calming environment that can reduce potential crisis triggers (more in chapter 16 [Managing Crises]).

How Do I Take Care of My Family and Myself?

Caregiver burnout is a very real concern for anyone who is involved in the care for someone with schizophrenia. The constant responsibilities and occasional crises, or other family and professional burdens, can lead to exhaustion, anger, anxiety, and depression. Burnout can have profoundly negative psychological and physical effects, and compromise caregiving ability.

Caregiving is not a sprint—it is a marathon! Sprinting all the time is a surefire recipe to burnout. The key to preventing caregiver burnout is taking care of yourself, and the rest of your family (see chapter 14 [Manual for Caregivers]). This includes regularly stepping away from caregiving duties, and doing things that are relaxing and revitalizing for you. It may seem impossible to take breaks, or you may feel indispensable, but that is rarely true. You need to figure how to accomplish this. This could mean enlisting the support of other family members, trusted friends, an agency, or a home health care aide.

Beyond the Help That I Provide, Where Else Can I Find More Assistance?

There is plenty of help available, in many forms, and at no or little cost. If you are no longer able to provide care at the level you would like to, or circumstances in your life have changed that no longer permit caregiving, then you need to reach out to the care team to figure out the best options. This may mean involving other family, but also other service providers. What's important is to know that you are not alone with this burden (see chapter 14 [Manual for Caregivers]).

Can I Say "No" to a Person with Schizophrenia If He or She Is Acting Inappropriately?

Yes. Just because a person has schizophrenia does not mean you have to accept "anything goes"—especially if these inappropriate behaviors represent safety threats to you or others in your home. Any interaction with you, as it is with any other family member, will have boundaries and rules. Of course, you will want to keep in mind the influence of schizophrenia on your loved one when establishing "house" rules and limits. It is best to work collaboratively with the patient to determine what expectations are appropriate, as well as how they will be enforced. As an example, you may choose not to allow smoking in the house or expect a certain standard of hygiene. What is useful in setting rules and expectations is that they are:

- *Concise* (not long and complicated rules)
- *Clear* (e.g., no smoking in the house)
- *Consequential* (not *every* behavior has to be rule-based; choose important behaviors. In other words, "don't sweat the small stuff")

As you think about setting rules and expectations, bear in mind that these behaviors need to be fair to all family members. Too many exceptions to the rules for the patient can create resentment in others. It is best to get the whole household involved in this process to avoid aggravating an already difficult situation.

What Is the Most Effective Way of Working with the Care (Treatment) Team?

Communication is key to working effectively with care teams. When care teams are provided necessary and *timely information*, they are better able to develop successful treatment plans, adjust the course of treatment as needed, and manage crises as they occur. If you are involved in patient's clinic visits, it is valuable to take notes to ensure that everyone is "on the same page" about the current treatment. It is also very useful to have a written record (e.g., a folder) of patient's treatment history, particularly in the event of emergencies.

Ideally, care teams will be equally communicative with you and the patient about important clinical decisions, and the thinking behind such changes. If this is not occurring, then you must raise this issue with the care team, or administrator of the program.

What about the Future When We Are No Longer Able to Provide Care or Housing, or Are No Longer Alive?

If you are young and healthy when your loved one is diagnosed with schizophrenia, stepping into a caregiving role may seem like the natural course of action. But schizophrenia is a lifelong disease; thus, as your loved one grows older, so will you. Nobody likes to think about being incapacitated or his or her eventual demise, but if you are the primary caregiver responsible for a loved one with complex set of needs, *planning* for the future is essential. At a minimum, consider your own future physical capabilities and financial situation. Other issues that need attention include income, housing, and care needs. This planning will probably require the use of documents such as powers of attorney, healthcare proxies, supplemental needs trusts, or guardianship arrangements (see chapter 14 [Manual for Caregivers]). Good sources for help include local nonprofit organizations, specialist attorneys, and the NAMI Planned Lifetime Assistance Network (PLAN). Not planning for the future is unfair to your loved one!

Final Thoughts About Schizophrenia:
- *It is a brain disorder*
- *It is not anyone's fault*
- *A person has schizophrenia, is not schizophrenic*
- *It can get better*
- *Attitude is everything!*

SECTION 2

What, Who, Why?

Core Clinical Features of Schizophrenia

What Is Not Schizophrenia?

Who Gets Schizophrenia?

How Is Schizophrenia Diagnosed?

What Is the Course and Prognosis of Schizophrenia?

CHAPTER 2

Core Clinical Features of Schizophrenia

The eye sees only what the mind is prepared to comprehend.
HENRI BERGSON, PHILOSOPHER AND NOBEL PRIZE WINNER

With a century-worth of observations and research, there is a consensus that schizophrenia is a syndrome with a set of core symptoms. Defining what is—and what is not—schizophrenia is important not only for the diagnostic process but also essential to determining the treatment plan and projected outcomes. Therefore, the proper recognition of symptoms and their relation to each other is of utmost importance.

Diagnosing schizophrenia is about identifying the core symptoms of the disease, while at the same time ruling out numerous other psychiatric or medical conditions that can present in similar ways.

Though no two patients will demonstrate the exact same symptoms, the most common signals of schizophrenia can be divided into three major categories (terms used by mental health professionals): positive symptoms, negative symptoms, and other symptoms.

POSITIVE SYMPTOMS

Do not be misled—these symptoms are not called positive because they are "good." Instead, think of the term as a "+" sign, meaning that there has been an addition of something that didn't exist before within a person's normal mental processes. *Delusions*, which are false beliefs, are positive symptoms. Likewise, *hallucinations* do not occur under normal circumstances; therefore, they are also referred to as positive symptoms.

Generally, when the term "psychosis" (loss of reality) is used, it refers to positive symptoms and severe thought disturbance.

Delusions are false beliefs, and sometimes seemingly irrational beliefs (about *any* idea), that are held despite evidence to the contrary. Delusions are held with conviction, and can be fixed (i.e., a single or a very few ideas). If false beliefs are held with much less conviction, they are referred to as *overvalued ideas*. Delusions are often at odds with the person's cultural and religious beliefs, or with the patient's level of education.

Delusions are categorized into a variety of types based on the general themes or content of delusional thinking (i.e., what the person is actually thinking) (Table 2.1). It is important to note that the *type* of delusion is generally not very important in managing the medical treatment of schizophrenia. However, since the content of delusional thinking can affect a patient's behavior, it becomes very important to clarify the nature of these delusions in order to interact with the patient. For example, a patient who believes that a family member is poisoning the food and consequently refuses to eat requires a different approach than a patient who believes that eating a certain food will make her weak. Also, one can experience more than one type of delusion occurring at the same time, or shift back and forth between different types. It is not uncommon for paranoid and grandiose delusions to coexist.

"I'm waiting for a sign so I can be ready."

"Ready for what?" I asked

"To go to them in the sky. I'm waiting for a sign."

"In the sky? You mean heaven?" I asked somewhat alarmed.

"I don't know who's there . . . aliens or something like that, but I have to wait for a sign."

"Do you know what this sign is supposed to be?"

"My DNA is going to change!"

"Change how?"

"I think it's supposed to untwist or something . . . but, I'll know . . . I'll feel it."

Hallucinations are another type of positive symptom. An example is hearing voices that are not real, *in addition* to hearing real speech. Thus, a hallucination is a false sensory experience that typically occurs in the *absence* of a stimulus (a trigger to stimulate sensation), and can involve any of our sensory systems. Seeing imaginary bugs on the floor or "ghosts" from the corner of the eye are examples of visual hallucinations. Persons experiencing hallucinations usually have normal hearing,

Table 2.1 Common Delusional Themes

Term	Description
Paranoid	Feels persecuted (harassed) or taken advantage of. May feel part of a vast conspiracy, or that there are special hidden messages within events or situation that others do not see or understand.
Grandiose	Convinced of having unique abilities, special knowledge, or special powers beyond normal; often feel superior to other people.
Referential thinking	The interpretation of common events or experiences—like TV shows, songs on the radio, or harmless gestures—as having personal relevance or representing specific codes. This form of thinking is often associated with paranoia.
Somatic	A belief that something is wrong with their bodies that cannot be seen or detected by others. These can include the idea that a cancer is growing within them regardless of medical results.
Erotomanic	Feeling convinced that famous, beautiful, rich, or an out-of-reach person has fallen in love with them. Acting on these beliefs can lead to troublesome behaviors, such as attempts to contact the imaginary "lover."
Thought broadcasting	The experience of having personal thoughts being transmitted out to the world, where they can be "read" by others. This can lead to isolation, anger and aggression, guilt, and attempting to "shut down" his or her thinking.
Thought insertion	A belief that unknown or imagined outside forces or beings are placing thoughts into their minds without their permission.
Delusions of passivity	The sensation that external forces or other people are controlling or interfering with the mind or body. This delusion is different from thought insertion wherein actions are not being controlled.
Jealous	The conviction that a partner or spouse is cheating. Such convictions can lead to relationship problems.

vision, and other sensations. Unlike delusional thinking wherein the person may "buy into" false ideas, hallucinations are often unwelcome and can be quite distressing!

The most common type of hallucination is auditory hallucinations, which are seen in 70–80% of patients. These hallucinations can vary in loudness, sometimes being so loud that patients have a hard time hearing anything else. Occasionally, the hallucinations become so "real" that patients start responding to them as if in a conversation (*talking back*), which can be quite disturbing to the people around. In general, hallucinations tend to be worse when one is by oneself, such as at bedtime.

"It's the voice of Angel Gabriel, I swear!" he said with eyes wide open and leaning forward.

I asked, "How do you know this, that it's Angel Gabriel?"

"He tells me all the time. One time he spelled out his name . . . that's how I know! Wouldn't you? One night when I was just lying there, I saw him standing at the end of my bed. I closed my eyes and prayed to Mother Mary. Then he left me and never came back, but he talks to me all the time. I'm okay with that."

"What does he say?" I wondered aloud.

"This and that, you know, this and that. . ." he said with a vacant smile.

The following is a listing of commonly reported hallucinations, categorized by the sensory system involved (Table 2.2).

Table 2.2 Types of Hallucinations

Sensory System	Commonly Reported Hallucinatory Experiences
Auditory (hearing)	Hearing specific sounds (e.g., knocking, creaking), vague whispers, single words (e.g., name of the patient) or sentences, single or multiple familiar or unfamiliar voices; comments on one's actions; conversation among speakers. Hallucinations can seem to arise from any conceivable object and direction, include from inside the body. There is a type of auditory hallucination referred to as *command* hallucination that can be distressing and even frightening. The person hears voices commanding specific actions, including harming others or self, or sexual acts.
Visual (vision)	Seeing shadows at the corner of eye, ghost-like images, seeing natural and unnatural objects without any real context. They can be partial or complete images of known or unknown persons, even complete scenes. Sometime the images can be very disturbing. Occasionally, the hallucinations are neutral or even pleasant.

Sensory System	Commonly Reported Hallucinatory Experiences
Somatosensory (physical sensations and balance)	These tend to be short-lived sensations of pain, electrical shocks, or something moving. Somewhat rare are hallucinations of body parts moving, including the brain. There can be sensations of shrinking body parts, as well as alterations in shape, color, or texture of body parts, including skin.
Olfactory (smell)	Usually unpleasant smells (e.g., feces, burning rubber, or flesh), or something identified as poison gas. Occasionally smells are pleasant like perfume or fruits. Unpleasant olfactory hallucinations, like body odor, can lead to excessive bathing and isolation.
Gustatory (taste)	Unusual tastes, particularly metallic or salty tastes, and occasionally bitterness. Certain medicines and foods can lead to such lingering unpleasant tastes, and need to be ruled out before assuming it is a hallucination.

DISORDERED THINKING

Beyond delusions and hallucinations, *disordered thinking* that results in compromised communication is another positive symptom.

Thinking difficulties are reflected in abnormal speech and writing, and also in strange behavior. This impairment can be so subtle that it does not appear to interfere with normal conversation (unless one is carefully paying attention to the speech pattern), or it can be so severe that the resulting speech is not comprehensible. When diagnosing schizophrenia, clinicians look at specific thought process disturbances (patterns of speech) as shown in Figure 2.1, and as outlined next (Table 2.3).

"How was the visit with your mom?"

"Fine . . . well not fine. . . she has new bloyfend."

"Did you mean boyfriend?" I said, trying to be helpful.

"Yeah . . . he's nice . . . kinda like Barbie, but worse. He tried to poke my mom and she gave him a kiss. Didn't kiss me . . . kissed the f . . . bloyfend. Dr. R, I do not want to go there no more . . . but the bus makes me go. I'm not putting change in that thing!"

What was noteworthy about this interaction is the presence of detectable meaning—of not enjoying the visit with his mother—but conveyed through the veil of a thought disorder.

Table 2.3 Types of Thought Disturbance

Technical Term	Patterns of Speech
Circumstantiality	The thoughts start off normally but start to wander off, including a great deal of detail. After a period of wandering, the person is *able to return to the original point* of the conversation. Generally, circumstantiality is observable only when the person is allowed to talk for a while, without interruption.
Tangentiality	In this case, the speech starts off normally, but quickly veers off into unrelated areas. The conversation *doesn't return to the original point*, regardless of how long the listener waits. When interrupted, patients tend to ask what the question was in the first place.
Loose associations	This pattern of speech becomes apparent rather quickly, because the listener is *unable to follow the train of thought*. The listener might have the urge to say, "I don't get it." The link between one thought and the next is unclear or nonexistent. When severe, speech becomes incomprehensible.
Thought blocking	This appears similar to the kind of thought interruption that we all occasionally experience when, in mid-sentence, the train of *thought is "lost"* due to distraction, but can be recovered with prompts. In the case of schizophrenia, the patient actually "loses" the thought and the conversation can no longer continue.
Flight of ideas	In this instance one fairly complete and coherent idea is followed by another idea, but with only a weak or no connection between the sequences of thoughts. The listener experiences it as a *zigzagging conversation*.
Neologism	This term comes from Greek (*neo* = new, *logos* = speech), refers to creating completely *new words* with meanings possibly only understood by the patient (e.g., "stupup").
Perseveration	It is the persistent or *excessive repetition* of an idea, phrase, or word, or even a gesture, beyond the initial stimulus (trigger). This persistent thinking or behavior is out of context and uninvited. The speech appears to sound like a "broken record."

Thought processes

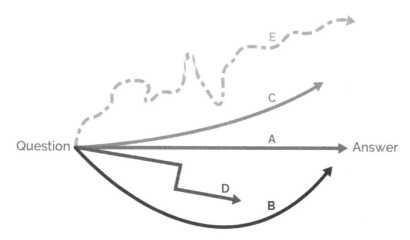

Figure 2.1 Thought Disorder Patterns: (A) Normal Thinking; (B) Circumstantiality; (C) Tangentiality; (D) Flight of Ideas; and (E) Loss of Associations

NEGATIVE SYMPTOMS

Similar to the idea of "+" in positive symptoms, think of "–" (minus symbol) in the case of negative symptoms, meaning that there has been a reduction or loss of normal functioning. For example, normal emotional expression (smiling, laughing, crying) may be reduced, resulting in a blank face.

Negative symptoms may be referred to as *primary* if they are brought about by schizophrenia or *secondary* if they result from some other problem such as depression or the treatment side effects.

> *With early intervention and consistent treatment, the management of positive and negative symptoms is often possible.*

Negative symptoms can be particularly bothersome to patients because these can interfere with important aspects of life involving feelings, pleasure, socialization, and work. They also tend to be less responsive to conventional treatment. Further, negative symptoms can worsen communication with the family, and make the patient appear very passive and lazy. However, with early intervention and consistent treatment, it is possible to manage these symptoms. Speak with your care team about the appropriate course of action for addressing any of the following primary negative symptoms (Table 2.4).

Table 2.4 Categories of Negative Symptoms

Technical Term	Observation in Patients
Alogia	Alogia refers to a loss of decreased amount of speech, with brief responses, often offering only "yes" or "no" answers to questions. For example: Q: Did you have lunch? A: Yes. Q: What did you have to eat? A: Food. Q: Did you have more than one thing? A: Yes. It is important to remember that this is not deliberate. Thus, communication requires patience on part of the listener.
Affective blunting	Expression of emotions (*affect*) is a normal means of communicating the state of the mind. A happy mind tends to show a happy face; sadness is accompanied by a sad face and slumped over appearance. However, patients with this particular problem tend to have a reduced range of facial expression and body movements, which may be classified as mild ("restricted"), moderate ("blunted") or severe ("flat"). Thus, a patient showing little emotion when receiving good or bad news is demonstrating affective blunting. In severe instances, a patient may be observed sitting in a chair, motionless and expressionless, staring off into space.
Avolition	Unfortunately, many patients are labeled as lazy, due to an apparent lack of interest in initiating or following through on tasks, and planning for the future. This lack of "get up and go" can be frustrating to both patient and family. It can also interfere with proper self-care, doing common chores like housekeeping, and keeping up with day-to-day activities.
Anhedonia	A common complaint patients have is the gradual decrease in pleasure experienced from previous hobbies or activities. Consequently, patients may perform their tasks in a mechanical, bored manner or stare at the television for hours on end with no indication of enjoyment. This inability to enjoy activities is distressing for everyone.
Asociality	There are many reasons why patients exhibit a tendency to isolate themselves from others, or exhibit a lack of interest in engaging with others. Sometimes, isolation is due to paranoia or intense hallucinations (positive symptoms). However, when "asociality" is not a consequence of positive symptoms, it is a primary negative symptom that occurs in roughly 25% of sufferers. For example, it is common to decline attending family gatherings, or to be off by themselves when there are people around. Families tend to accept this behavior more easily since it is not very troublesome.

OTHER SYMPTOMS IN SCHIZOPHRENIA

Beyond the classic positive and negative symptoms that are associated with this disease, other common symptoms may be detected in patients, and taken into account when determining the diagnosis. Broadly, these symptoms fall into four categories: emotional disturbances, behavioral disturbances, cognitive abnormalities, and neurological abnormalities.

Emotional Disturbances

Unlike other mood disorders, such as depression, there is no "cut-and-dried" emotional disturbance that is typical of schizophrenia. Instead, a wide variety of abnormal emotional states may occur, everything from anxiety to elation to depression. In fact, the ecstatic states observed in some patients are so extreme as to cause them to believe they're undergoing powerful religious experiences.

Patients with schizophrenia may also display what is known as *inappropriate affect*, or the appearance of disconnect between thoughts or speech, and display of emotions. Patients experiencing this symptom may grin when describing sad circumstances or even burst into tears while sharing amusing stories.

Behavioral Disturbances

Apart from emotional symptoms, many patients have behavioral abnormalities that are not necessarily related to underlying delusions or hallucinations. Some common behaviors are described here, along with the terms you may hear your doctors using:

- Odd postures or poses (*posturing*). For example, standing on one leg for no obvious reason.
- Goal-driven actions that are carried out in an odd fashion (*mannerisms*). For example, repeatedly adjusting eyeglasses by removing them, turning them over, and putting them on. The patient is able to tell you what he's doing, but not necessarily why.
- Repeated movements that appear regular but lack a purpose, as in the case of tapping or rocking (*stereotypies*).
- The imitation of movements performed by others (*echopraxia*). For example, if I touch my chin, the patient mirrors the movement, no matter how many times I repeat the action.
- The imitation of words used or statements made by others (*echolalia*). Similar to echopraxia, but with words. For example, if I say,

"Have a good day!" the patient will echo it, and say "Have a good day!" no matter the number of times I say it.
- Excited, *aimless* motor activity (*catatonic excitement*).
- The appearance of motionlessness (*catatonic stupor*), generally for a long period of time.

Cognitive Abnormalities

Cognition refers to the processes of awareness, recognizing the environment, reasoning, memory, and problem solving. Some patients are easily distracted or unable to stay focused, and miss the point of conversations. Memory problems can show up as inaccurate recall of facts, stories, or ideas. There can be trouble with language such as loss of vocabulary, speech output, and poor sentence construction. Planning ahead or the proper sequencing of actions can be compromised.

Neurological Abnormalities

To be clear, while patients with schizophrenia often exhibit subtle neurological disturbances that point to a biological basis for the disease, these signs are not currently considered specific enough help with the diagnostic process. As a result, these symptoms are referred to as *soft signs*. Examples include disturbances in *motor coordination* (gait, balance, coordination, and muscle tone) and *sensory integration* (such as the ability to sense the position of the body in space or to perceive the material properties of an object).

SUMMARY

- The origin of the word "schizophrenia" refers to "split mind," but that is an inaccurate picture of the condition. Today, schizophrenia is defined by the presence of a specific set of signs and symptoms.
- No two patients experience the same set of symptoms.
- "Positive" symptoms represent something *added* to the patient's normal mental functioning and commonly include delusions and hallucinations.
- "Negative" symptoms get their name from a lessening or loss of normal mental functioning, and are represented by the 5 "As"— alogia, affective blunting, avolition, anhedonia, and asociality.
- Other symptoms experienced by patients include emotional disturbances, behavioral disturbances, cognitive abnormalities, and neurological abnormalities.

CHAPTER 3

What Is Not Schizophrenia?

They certainly give very strange names to diseases.
PLATO, GREEK PHILOSOPHER (428–347 BCE)

B ecause no definitive diagnostic test exists for schizophrenia, identifying the disorder is often achieved as much by ruling out other similar conditions as it is by proving that it is schizophrenia. You probably haven't heard the names of most of these conditions, but they occur with sufficient frequency that they have to be considered in the *differential diagnosis* (list of possible diagnoses).

Ruling out conditions with similar symptoms as schizophrenia is an essential part of the diagnostic process.

If you or a relative is experiencing symptoms that point toward schizophrenia, expect that your medical team will take into consideration all of the following conditions as part of the diagnostic process. Doing so is an essential part of both establishing a diagnosis of schizophrenia and developing the specific, individual treatment plan that is most likely to lead to positive outcomes.

OTHER PSYCHIATRIC DISORDERS

"Psychosis" is a term with specific meaning in the mental health community. It means *loss of contact with reality*, such as delusions, hallucinations, and irrational thinking and behaviors. From a medical standpoint, psychosis itself is not a diagnosis. Instead, it is best thought of as a clinical condition, similar to having a fever. In the same way that fever reflects an ongoing disturbance of the body's ability to regulate its temperature, psychosis reflects dysfunction within the brain. Just as fever can have many causes, so too can psychosis. Therefore, having psychosis does not necessarily mean it is schizophrenia! There are many psychiatric disorders in which psychosis occurs; these possibilities need to be ruled out before assigning the diagnosis of schizophrenia.

Brief Psychotic Disorder

This diagnosis may be given if a patient experiences short-lived psychotic symptoms that occur for less than one month in duration, and emerges in relation to a significant psychosocial stressor. The term "reactive psychosis" has also been used to describe such cases. This may progress to full schizophrenia if symptoms persist, and go on to meet the clinical definitions of the disease.

Schizophreniform Disorder

If schizophrenia-like symptoms persist for more than one month, and less than the six months that is required for a full diagnosis of schizophrenia, the condition is referred to as schizophreniform disorder. This disorder typically includes a rapid onset, perplexity, or other confusion, and a relatively intact emotional expression (affect). If this condition progresses beyond six months, it's likely to be schizophrenia.

Schizoaffective Disorder

Patients with schizoaffective disorder experience both the symptoms of schizophrenia (including hallucinations and delusions) and mood disorders (e.g., mania and depression). However, it is not a simple issue of someone with schizophrenia having episodes of depression at the same time; schizoaffective appears to be a separate condition altogether. The DSM-5 approaches schizoaffective disorder from a life course basis. Patients who only experience psychotic symptoms during mood episodes are now more likely to be diagnosed as having "mood disorders with psychotic features," saving the label of schizoaffective disorder for those whose symptoms include at least a two-week period of psychosis *without* major mood symptoms and whose mood episodes have existed during a substantive portion of the course of illness. This complicated definition can be derived only if sufficient time has passed to allow proper observation of the illness course. The treatment of this condition is not very different from that of schizophrenia.

Delusional Disorder

This disorder is characterized by the presence of delusions (these can be the same types as noted earlier), but have no other significant psychosis or prominent negative symptoms. Again, differentiating between delusional disorder and schizophrenia requires careful observation and clinical acumen.

Mood Disorders

Though schizophrenia patients may experience mood symptoms like depression and mania, it is the presence of psychotic symptoms like delusions and hallucinations that generally differentiate schizophrenia from mood disorders.

Bipolar Disorder

Bipolar disorder, used to be referred to as *manic-depressive disorder*, is a condition in which patients experience periods of abnormally high moods (*mania* or *manic episodes*) alternating with periods of abnormally low moods (depression or depressive episodes). While all people experience the usual highs and lows associated with daily life, those with bipolar disorder experience these shifts more intensely. At their highest points, sufferers may feel so invincible that they stay up for days on end or engage in extreme risk-taking behaviors. At their lowest, they may sink into such deep depressions that they become suicidal. Grandiose and paranoid delusions can occur in bipolar disorder.

Schizotypal Personality Disorder

Though schizotypal personality disorder may sound similar to schizophrenia, its symptoms tend to be much less severe, with no clear psychosis. Typically viewed by others as being eccentric, these patients experience difficulties forming and maintaining close relationships.

Schizoid Personality Disorder

Patients with schizoid personality disorder tend to detach from interpersonal relationships and show low levels of emotion, expressiveness, and responsiveness that might be expected in a given situation. As a result, those with this condition are often viewed as being distant or unemotional, though they generally lack the delusions and hallucinations.

Paranoid Personality Disorder

The primary characteristic of paranoid personality disorder sufferers is, as you might expect, is suspiciousness. Patients with this condition have trouble forming relationships with others, given their natural inclination to view others with distrust or to irrationally suspect that others are acting against them.

Borderline Personality Disorder

This condition is marked by impulsivity, which can manifest in risk-taking behaviors, instability of mood, intense shifts in personal relationships, self-mutilation, or suicidal thoughts. The intensity of these symptoms can cause mental health professionals to suspect schizophrenia, though further examination will reveal the absence of the persistent, organized delusions and hallucinations that often lead to a schizophrenia diagnosis.

Antisocial Personality Disorder

This term is often confused with the common meaning of the term antisocial—unsociable. However, antisocial personality disorder has specific meaning in psychiatry. Patients with this condition actively antagonize and mistreat others, seemingly with no regard for their rights or for the law in general. Consequently, they may have problems with drug and alcohol use, as well as legal troubles that can be so severe as to leave them incapable of fulfilling normal family and work responsibilities. Because asociality is often a prominent symptom experienced by schizophrenia sufferers, this similar condition must be ruled out.

Dissociative Identity Disorder

Although schizophrenia and dissociative identity disorder (also known as *multiple personality disorder*) are often confused, they are not the same. Schizophrenia is a disorder of the brain that is characterized by the presence of both delusions and hallucinations. Patients with dissociative identity disorder often have histories of traumatic events, such as physical or sexual abuse. Hallucinations are present in only about one-third of these patients.

Autism Spectrum Disorders

Disorders of brain development such as autism can occasionally be mistaken for schizophrenia. Patients with autism also have difficulties in initiating and maintaining social relationships, and have repetitive behaviors and unusual use of language similar to schizophrenia. However, autism begins much earlier, that is, in early childhood; positive symptoms, such as delusions and hallucinations, are uncommon.

MEDICAL CONDITIONS

Besides the psychiatric disorders described earlier, medical conditions must also be ruled out because they can present with symptoms that mimic schizophrenia. We use a mnemonic—TACTICS MDS USE—to help us remember the many, many medical and nonmedical conditions to rule out before assigning the diagnosis of schizophrenia (Table 3.1).

Depending on the severity of your condition and the symptoms you display, your care team may want to test you for several of these disorders or none at all.

Table 3.1 Differential Diagnosis of Schizophrenia (*TACTICS MDS USE*)

Category	Common Examples
Trauma	Head or brain injury
Autoimmune disorders	Rheumatic fever, multiple sclerosis (MS)
Cytogenetic/congenital disorders	Genetic/chromosomal disorders such as 22q deletion syndrome
Toxic/substance-induced disorders	Alcohol, anxiolytics (e.g., diazepam), marijuana, cocaine, hallucinogens (e.g., LSD), hypnotics, inhalants, opioids, PCP, ketamine, sedatives, and other stimulants
Iatrogenic disorders	Steroids, antimalarials
Cerebrovascular disorders	Hydrocephalus
Space-occupying disorders	Brain tumors
Metabolic disorders	Wilson's disease
Dietary disorders	Pellagra (vitamin B_3 deficiency) and pernicious anemia (vitamin B_{12} deficiency)
Sepsis/infective disorders	Encephalitis
Unknown/degenerative/demyelinating disorders	Multiple sclerosis
Seizure disorders	Temporal lobe epilepsy, in particular
Endocrine disorders	Addison's disease, Cushing's syndrome, hyperthyroidism, hypothyroidism, and hyperparathyroidism

Street or Prescription Drug Abuse

The effects of street or prescription drug use may imitate the symptoms of schizophrenia. That said, the actual connections between the two are not entirely clear, though researchers have, in recent years, suggested a possible causative relationship between heavy marijuana use and the development of schizophrenia. However, the data underlying this assertion is weak at best, and hard data implicating the use of marijuana, LSD, PCP, or any other street or prescription medication in the onset of schizophrenia is actively debated.

> *Data implicating the use of marijuana, LSD, PCP, or any other street or prescription medication in the onset of schizophrenia is currently a matter of debate.*

What we do know about the relationship between drug use and schizophrenia is that the chronic use of mind-altering drugs can damage the parts of the brain associated with intellectual function and memory, potentially aggravating the symptoms of a person with preexisting schizophrenia. At the same time, we know that it is common for those developing the earliest symptoms of schizophrenia to seek out drug usage as a means to either explain away or self-medicate their initially frightening symptoms. This contributes to the "chicken and egg" scenario of which came first—the drug use or the schizophrenia.

Although our understanding of drug use as a causative agent in the development of schizophrenia is incomplete, we do know that ongoing drug usage can complicate treatment and lead to poorer outcomes for patients. As a result, it is important for mental health professionals to identify the use of alcohol, anxiolytics (e.g., diazepam), marijuana, cocaine, hallucinogens (e.g., LSD), hypnotics, inhalants, opioids, PCP, ketamine, sedatives, and other stimulants in patients with schizophrenia in order to formulate an appropriate treatment plan.

CULTURALLY SANCTIONED PSYCHOTIC BEHAVIOR

Interestingly, symptoms that seem to suggest schizophrenia may not be linked to a disease or disorder at all. They may, in fact, be the result of culturally accepted social practices. Take, for example, people who hear voices compelling them to speak in tongues during religious ceremonies. While these experiences or beliefs might seem to point to a diagnosis of brief psychotic disorder or even schizophrenia (depending on their duration and severity), the fact that their community or circumstances do not consider them abnormal must be taken into account.

Because psychotic syndromes with unique clinical features have been described in a variety of cultures worldwide, clinicians carefully exclude these seemingly psychotic behaviors from diagnostically relevant symptoms. While in general, psychiatric symptoms can be differentiated from culturally sanctioned behaviors and sorted into one or another DSM-V diagnostic category, the potential impact of culture on phenomena such as hallucinations, delusions, or unusual behaviors should not be minimized or dismissed by your clinical team.

SUMMARY

- Because no definitive test for schizophrenia exists, clinicians must often rely on ruling out other similar disorders in order to arrive at a diagnosis.
- Other psychotic disorders, such as brief psychotic disorder, schizophreniform disorder, schizoaffective disorder and delusional disorder, are prime candidates for the presentation of overlapping symptoms.
- The highs and lows of bipolar disorder can also cause mental health professionals to mistake this mood disorder for schizophrenia.
- Personality disorders—including schizoid personality disorder, schizotypal personality disorder and paranoid personality disorder, among others—must also be considered, especially if suspected schizophrenia presents early in life.
- Dissociative identity disorder (commonly referred to as "multiple personality disorder") is a distinct condition that may be confused with schizophrenia.
- A number of different medical conditions may present with symptoms similar to schizophrenia. Clinical professionals may choose to rule out some or all of these diseases through medical testing, depending on the symptoms the patient is experiencing.
- Although it is currently unclear whether street or prescription drug use can cause schizophrenia, identifying the usage of these substances is a critical part of formulating an appropriate treatment plan.
- Culturally sanctioned psychotic behaviors (e.g., hearing voices that compel a participant in a religious ceremony to speak in tongues) are not indicative of schizophrenia and must be ruled out based on their acceptance within the patient's community.

CHAPTER 4

Who Gets Schizophrenia?

Sometimes our fate is different from the one we imagined for ourselves.

JEAN KWOK, *GIRL IN TRANSLATION*

Your first thought upon hearing a schizophrenia diagnosis handed to you or your relative might well be, "Why me (or my loved one)?" It is very understandable to feel upset about having the course of your life altered in such a dramatic way. After all, nobody wants to be stuck with a disease that is so grossly misunderstood by the general public, and whose sufferers face so much prejudice and stigma throughout the course of their lives.

Learning about who is at risk for schizophrenia may help you feel less alone as you confront your diagnosis.

Unfortunately, answers to the question "Why me?" are not always easy to come by. As we'll discuss in the next section of this book, our understanding of schizophrenia's causes remains incomplete. Despite this, researchers have been able to identify a series of risk factors that could influence who might develop schizophrenia. Learning about these potential indicators may allow you to assess your own (or your relative's) risk level and identify situations where extra monitoring may be beneficial in the future. It can also help you to feel less alone as you confront the prospect of a schizophrenia diagnosis for you or your relative.

DEFINITIONS

Before we dive into the risk factors and trends that seem to influence the diagnosis of schizophrenia, it is useful to be familiar with some key terms, as you will see these in research articles and books on the topic:

Incidence refers to the number of people *newly* diagnosed with a specific condition during a specific period of time (usually a year). With regard to schizophrenia, the incidence is approximately 3 to 6 individuals for a group of 10,000 people. In other words, the overall risk of being diagnosed with schizophrenia is quite low, but that risk is affected by factors such as family history.

Prevalence refers to the notion of how many persons in total with a given diagnosis exist in a given population, at a specific time (usually a year). The latest research indicates that between 4 and 7 individuals out of a 1,000 people has schizophrenia. As a conservative estimate, there are 20 million individuals worldwide with schizophrenia, including 2.2 million in the United States. It is clear that schizophrenia is not an uncommon condition.

Lifetime prevalence is not a straightforward notion; it combines the concept of prevalence with that of risk of being diagnosed with the condition at *any* time during a person's life. In other words, it is another way of assessing risk within a population. Specifically, it is an estimate of individuals who will develop the disorder at *some point during their lifetime* within a specific population. Current research indicates a lifetime prevalence for schizophrenia is 0.5%, lower than the commonly quoted 1%.

RISK FACTORS

The following risk factors may all influence a person's likelihood of being diagnosed with schizophrenia, though it is important to remember that none of these factors are strong enough alone to guarantee the development of the disease.

Age

According to well-established research, we know that schizophrenia is most likely to affect people between ages 17 and 35, and that its onset tends to occur earlier in men than women. However, not all newly diagnosed cases fall into this range. Schizophrenia can begin in children as young as 5 or in adults in their 50s, 60s, and 70s. That being said, childhood onset is extremely rare. Only one in 40,000 children will be diagnosed with schizophrenia, and just one in 100 adults who have been diagnosed experienced schizophrenic symptoms before reaching age 13.

Sex

As mentioned earlier, men typically experience an earlier onset of schizophrenia than women, typically by a margin of five years (although, interestingly, late-onset schizophrenia is more commonly diagnosed in women than in men). These are not the only sex-specific differences that exist with regards to schizophrenia. Indeed, clinical presentation, treatment response, and long-term outcomes all vary between men and women as well.

Women, for example, tend to experience a more rapid onset of symptoms than men. When symptoms do occur, men tend to display more negative symptoms than women, who typically present with depressed mood and paranoia, and experience a higher level of functioning when ill. It is not entirely clear why, but women also tend to respond better to initial treatment, though they often exhibit more side effects than men. As a result, men tend to have poorer outcomes than women, although women may be plagued by ongoing hormonal fluctuations that can affect symptom severity.

Some researchers theorize that these differences are due to biological factors, like the presence of the hormone *estrogen* in women. Others suggest that environmental factors, such as better socialization in women, play a contributing role. But regardless of the reason, it is important to note that being a man does not doom a sufferer to treatment failure. Both men and women are capable of experiencing symptom relief—if not outright remission—if they actively follow prescribed treatment plans in order to manage their condition.

Family History

Given that many researchers believe the cause of schizophrenia lies, at least in part, in our genes, it is natural for those who have a family history of the disease to be concerned about their chances of developing the condition. Fortunately, while having relatives with schizophrenia increases your own chances of being diagnosed with the disease, it is still far from a sure thing. What we know right now is that, if one parent has schizophrenia, the child's risk of having the disease is about 10%. When both parents suffer, the child's risk increases to 30–46%. If one of identical twins has the condition, the risk that the other will increase to about 40%. If the twins are fraternal (i.e., not identical), there is a 10–17% chance that the undiagnosed twin will go on to develop schizophrenia, the same as other siblings.

While having relatives with schizophrenia increases your own chances of being diagnosed with the disease, it is still far from a sure thing.

Again, even if you have a close relative or relatives with schizophrenia, there is no guarantee that you'll ever develop the disease yourself. That said, you should use your awareness of these risk factors to monitor yourself or your children for early warning signs and symptoms. As a general rule, the earlier schizophrenia is detected, the better the odds of successful treatment outcomes. If you are at a higher risk for developing the condition based on these and other factors, early vigilance is critical.

Ethnicity, Race, and Geographic Location

In the past, researchers in the United States believed that rates of schizophrenia were higher in black people than in white people. A large epidemiological study known as the Epidemiologic Catchment Area study conducted from 1980 to 1985 did not, however, find significant differences between the two groups.

Immigration

Interestingly, immigrants appear to be at a heightened risk of developing schizophrenia, as in the case of the Afro-Cuban immigrants to the United Kingdom. While some researchers believe that this is a natural consequence of the stress associated with migration, others hold that the presence of mental illness itself promotes migration.

Environment

Beyond age, gender, family history, and immigration status, there are several biological and environmental factors that are found to increase the risk of developing schizophrenia, although their exact pathogenic mechanisms have not yet been deciphered. It is important to remember that the following factors are risk indicators, not predictors of developing schizophrenia!

Perinatal (around Birth) Complications
About 25% of patients (most often males) have a history of variety of pregnancy and birth complications. It is suggested that birth complications may increase the risk of subtle brain injury due to

reduced oxygen at that time. Prenatal (before birth) exposure to influenza during the second trimester, nutritional deficiencies, and maternal starvation (as a result of poverty or eating disorders) also increase the risk of the child eventually being diagnosed with schizophrenia. Maternal stress may also play a role, as the risk of developing schizophrenia (or a related disorder) was 67% greater among the children of mothers who experienced the death of a close family member during the first trimester.

Season of Birth
It appears that *when* one is born may slightly impact the risk for schizophrenia. Compared to people born in summer or fall seasons, late winter and early spring appear to be the riskier seasons. Since the seasons are opposite in the two hemispheres, January through April are somewhat riskier months in the Northern Hemisphere, and July through September in the Southern Hemisphere. Researchers theorize that higher rates of *viral infections* during the winter months may account for these seasonal differences.

Paternal Age
There is evidence that being born to older fathers might slightly increase risk for schizophrenia. This may be related to an increased likelihood of gene mutations in relation to advanced paternal age.

Being Born in Urban Areas
There is evidence that schizophrenia patients are more likely to be born in inner-city neighborhoods. There is little support for the earlier view that this association is due to the schizophrenia patients' "drifting" to inner-city areas because of the negative consequences of the illness. Rather, it is likely that the stress, social alienation, and fragmentation in urban areas may increase risk for the illness.

It is worth noting again that these are only risk factors that suggest a higher likelihood of developing schizophrenia; they are not diagnostic in and of themselves. For instance, it is certainly possible to be born in January or have an older father and not go on to develop schizophrenia. While these risk factors paint an interesting picture of likely schizophrenia sufferers and give researchers plenty of avenues to explore, it is possible to develop schizophrenia in their absence, just as it is possible to avoid diagnosis altogether when they are present.

SUMMARY

- Although known risk factors exist for schizophrenia, their presence alone is not enough to definitively predict eventual diagnosis.
- The majority of patients are diagnosed with schizophrenia between ages 17 and 35, although diagnosis can occur as early as age 5 and as late as a patient's 50s, 60s or 70s.
- Men typically experience an earlier onset of the disease and more negative symptoms, while women generally enjoy better treatment outcomes, but more side effects.
- Having a parent or twin diagnosed with schizophrenia increases your chances of developing the disease by 10–46%, depending on the closeness of blood relationship.
- Immigration appears to increase the risk of developing schizophrenia, though the mechanism behind this effect is currently unclear.
- Perinatal complications, season of birth, and greater paternal age may all signal a greater risk of developing schizophrenia.

CHAPTER 5

How Is Schizophrenia Diagnosed?

Early diagnosis is so important because the earlier a mental illness can be detected, diagnosed and treatment can begin, the better off that person can be for the rest of his or her life.
ROSALYNN CARTER, WIFE OF FORMER PRESIDENT JIMMY CARTER

Most of us are familiar with the general process of receiving a medical diagnosis. You experience symptoms, describe them to a doctor, and receive both a diagnosis and the treatment options that are appropriate for your condition. This process is used to identify and remedy everything from strep throat to kidney stones, and from typhoid fever to skin cancer and more.

Arriving at the diagnosis of schizophrenia is, unfortunately, rarely straightforward. Unlike the medical conditions listed earlier, schizophrenia has no defining features that are unique to the condition alone. There is no laboratory test or a single clinical feature that can point toward a diagnosis of schizophrenia, which means that mental health professionals must solely rely on signs and symptoms. Since there are many different mental disorders that exhibit the same symptoms as seen in schizophrenia, all the other conditions should be ruled out before a handing out a life-altering diagnosis of schizophrenia. Thus, it is very important that patients and their families cooperate with mental health professionals by providing accurate information, and not ignore or "hide" or minimize symptoms. This will only delay arriving at the correct diagnosis, and consequently delay proper treatment.

There is no laboratory test or a single clinical feature that can point toward a diagnosis of schizophrenia, which means that mental health professionals must solely rely on signs and symptoms alone.

Given these challenges, the mental health community has evolved a systematic process that must be followed before a diagnosis of schizophrenia can be given. Whether you suspect a relative is experiencing the condition or you're in the middle of the diagnostic process yourself, the following description should help you get insight into what doctors are looking for before assigning this challenging label.

BEGINNING THE DIAGNOSTIC PROCESS

Despite the challenges associated with diagnosing schizophrenia, a definitive diagnosis is critically important and allows sufferers to begin exploring treatment options as well as making appropriate plans for the future.

Persons suspected of having schizophrenia come to the attention of mental health professionals in a number of different ways, and under a variety of circumstances. Thus, it could be someone brought in by relatives or friends because of changes in thinking or behavior, to patients who have progressed to a severely symptomatic state before seeking medical intervention. While it is easier to diagnose schizophrenia in patients who are already in the later stages of the disease, beginning the diagnostic process quickly will ultimately lead to better treatment outcomes.

If you or a relative experience behavioral changes that raise the suspicion of a mental illness, particularly schizophrenia, seek professional assistance as soon as possible. There are varieties of behavioral changes, sometimes subtle, that tend to precede the onset of clinical schizophrenia, called *prodromal symptoms*. Prodromal means that these symptoms may occur in patients before the illness fully develops. Commonly observed prodromal symptoms are:

- Social withdrawal and an increased tendency to remain alone
- A decline in performance at school or work
- Loss of motivation and an inability to concentrate
- Increased irritability, depression, or anxiety
- Suspiciousness
- Neglect of physical appearance
- Changes in sleep patterns

It is important to recognize that any one of the behavioral changes mentioned earlier, or all of them, can be explained by a wide variety of medical, psychiatric, or substance abuse issues. That is why it is important to obtain a proper evaluation to rule out those other conditions before assuming it is necessarily the onset of schizophrenia.

PSYCHIATRIC EVALUATION

While gathering information on the symptoms a patient has been experiencing, the mental health professional will conduct what's known as a psychiatric assessment, which includes the taking of the complete history and the assessment of current level of psychiatric functioning. During this examination, the clinician has four primary goals:

- To determine whether the patient is a danger to himself or herself or others
- To determine whether the patient is using illicit substances that could contribute to or complicate the diagnosis of schizophrenia
- To determine whether the patient is compliant with any treatment protocols that have already been established
- To determine whether there are any ongoing medical problems that could influence the process of diagnosis and treatment

CLINICAL HISTORY

Getting a good history is a critical part of initiating a schizophrenia diagnosis. In many situations, though, this can be challenging, as patients may not be thinking clearly, may forget past experiences, or find themselves overcome with anxiety at the prospect of medical intervention. To get a more complete picture of the patient's troubles, clinicians may ask a variety of questions to family members and close friends. The specific questions the clinician asks you or your relative as part of the patient history interview may vary, but the ultimate goal of gathering this information is to understand both the patient's current experience and the trajectory of symptoms that led him or her to seek medical intervention. Examples of question include:

- What symptoms are you experiencing today?
- How long have you been experiencing these symptoms?
- How often do these symptoms occur?
- Have you taken any substances, such as marijuana or cocaine, which could be affecting your symptoms?
- Are you thinking about hurting yourself or others?
- Have you ever been diagnosed with depression or experienced depressive thoughts?
- How frequently do you drink alcohol?
- Are the symptoms you're experiencing affecting your ability to take care of yourself, go to work, or attend school?

The clinician who conducts the interview listens to both the content of the responses and the way they're delivered. In the event that a patient is not able to communicate verbally, doctors may find it sufficient to simply observe how the patient behaves in the clinical setting in order to identify different physical behaviors that may point toward a diagnosis of schizophrenia.

Evaluating the patient alone may provide all the information needed to consider a diagnosis of schizophrenia, or it may not be entirely helpful depending on his or her level of communication and cooperation. In most instances, talking to relatives and friends during the evaluation process can help establish the true clinical picture.

MENTAL STATUS EXAMINATION

The second half of the psychiatric evaluation process is the *mental status examination*, which aims to determine the current state of the patient's thought processes, overall mood, memory function, and more. This process may seem lengthy, and many questions may appear irrelevant at the moment. However, there are good reasons why a thorough evaluation requires present history and symptoms, past history, family history, medical history, as well as developmental history (childhood, schooling, etc.). This "360 degree" view of the person's mental state provides valuable diagnostic clues and specific treatment objectives. A comprehensive evaluation is the best bet against a *diagnostic error*.

MEDICAL TESTING

Depending on the results of the psychiatric evaluation, clinicians may conduct a physical exam and order medical tests to help rule out conditions that could cause similar symptoms as schizophrenia, including brain tumors, seizure disorders, thyroid conditions, and metabolic disorders. The following are a few of the medical tests that may be ordered as part of the diagnostic process:

- Urine drug/toxicology screen
- Complete blood count (CBC)
- Kidney and liver function tests
- Electrolyte level testing (glucose, sodium, potassium, and others)
- Thyroid function testing
- Brain imaging (CT or MRI)
- Sleep-deprived EEG (a special variation of EEG to rule out epilepsy)

After ruling out other conditions that may present as schizophrenia, the clinician has to determine whether the clinical picture fits standard diagnostic criteria. The most commonly system in the United States (and some other countries) is *The Diagnostic and Statistical Manual of Mental Disorders*, fifth edition (American Psychiatric Association, 2013). The other widely used system is the *International Classification of Diseases* (ICD) guidelines developed by World Health Organization (WHO).

DSM-5 DIAGNOSTIC CRITERIA

- Two or more of the following symptoms must be present for a significant portion of time during a one-month period:
  - Delusions
  - Hallucinations
  - Disorganized speech
  - Catatonia or other grossly abnormal psychomotor behavior
  - Negative symptoms, including flat affect or asociality
- Significant decreased function at work, in interpersonal relations, or in self-care
- At least one month of active symptoms (unless successfully treated) and at least six months of all symptoms (including prodromal, active, and residual characteristics)
- Does not meet criteria for schizoaffective disorder, and symptoms of psychosis are not caused by substance abuse, or another medical condition.

ICD-10

Current ICD-10 criteria require the presence, for at least one month, of one well-defined symptom from the following group:

- Thought disturbance (thought echo, insertion, withdrawal, or broadcasting)
- Delusions of passivity
- Persistent delusions
- Auditory hallucinations

Or, two or more symptoms from the following group *if the preceding symptoms are absent* or not clear-cut:

- Persistent hallucinations
- Disturbance in thought processing (e.g., derailment, irrelevant speech, or neologisms)
- Catatonic behavior

- Negative symptoms
- Significant and consistent changes in behavior (e.g., loss of interest, social withdrawal)

GETTING A SECOND OPINION

Receiving a diagnosis of schizophrenia is a life-disrupting event. And while it is a positive step for those patients who will benefit from immediate treatment, it can—understandably—also cause feelings of anxiety, fear, and even anger. Nobody likes the idea of being labeled as having schizophrenia by the medical system or by society at large, so it is natural to want to seek a second (or third, or fourth) opinion for confirmation.

That said, pursuing a second opinion isn't a process that should be undertaken lightly. Not only can the process be expensive (depending on your insurance coverage), it can set back the treatment clock by requiring additional time to revisit the diagnostic process, which may not be in your best interest.

When Should You Seek a Second Opinion?

- When your current provider won't give you a firm diagnosis or treatment plan after an adequate assessment period
- When you have doubts about your doctor or questions that haven't been answered satisfactorily
- If you show no signs of improvement under your current provider's care
- When you think it might be helpful to have a fresh set of eyes take a look at the problem
- When you want to take advantage of experimental treatments being offered by different providers

If you do decide to pursue this option, there are a number of different ways to find a new care team. Your current doctor or medical system may be able to refer you to a clinician who is better suited to your needs. Your city may put together "best doctor" lists that include psychiatric specialists. Or, you may even be able to speak with the families of other sufferers or your local National Alliance on Mental Illness chapter, a support organization, for referrals to the appropriate mental health professionals.

As you seek alternative perspectives on your condition, do your best to be respectful of both your current doctors and any new professionals you interact with. Although being diagnosed with schizophrenia can be frustrating, try to remember the members of your care team are doing their best to get you the treatment and resources you need.

SUMMARY

- Diagnosing schizophrenia is not a straightforward process. There are no symptoms or medical tests that can conclusively prove schizophrenia.
- The diagnostic process involves a psychiatric evaluation consisting of a patient interview and mental status examination.
- Schizophrenia symptoms must be present for a minimum of six months to receive a diagnosis. Symptoms that are present for less than one month may be diagnosed as brief psychotic disorder, while symptoms that are present for one to five months may be labeled schizophreniform disorder.
- Standardized criteria for diagnosing schizophrenia are provided by the *Diagnostic and Statistical Manual of Mental Disorders* (DSM) and *International Classification of Diseases* (ICD).

CHAPTER 6

What Is the Course and Prognosis of Schizophrenia?

> Life can only be understood backwards; but it must be lived forwards.
>
> SØREN KIERKEGAARD, PHILOSOPHER

Once a diagnosis of schizophrenia has been made, patients and their families all want to know what the probable outcome is. What will happen next? Will the symptoms ever go away? Are they destined to a life of impairment or complete disability? Answers to these questions are important to making informed life choices and determining treatment strategies.

Understanding the likely course of schizophrenia is helpful in making informed life choices and identifying the best possible treatments.

Unfortunately, there is no clear-cut way to determining who will experience only one episode of symptoms, or who will go on to become chronically disabled, or will have a middling course of illness. Forming a prognosis (from a Latin word which means "prediction") is a process, and rarely can it be determined at the very onset of illness. Many decades of observation and research about the course of illness have provided enough insights to put one myth to rest—that schizophrenia is a "one-size-fits-all" diagnosis that necessarily results in incapacitation.

COURSE OF THE DISEASE

Just as no two patients with schizophrenia will present with the same set of symptoms, no two sufferers will experience the same disease course. Differences in age at onset of symptoms, severity of symptoms, response

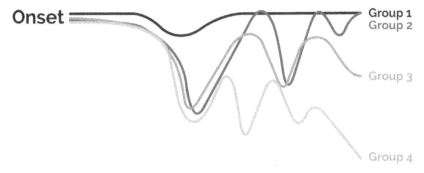

Figure 6.1 Course of Schizophrenia

to treatment, and several other factors influence the path an individual patient's disease will follow. In broad terms, there are four patterns to the course of illness:

- *Group 1* patient experiences a single episode of symptoms, fully recovers, and has no lasting impairment.
- *Group 2* patient undergoes a series of symptomatic periods, but recovers with minimal or no impairment between these episodes.
- *Group 3* patient experiences some level of impairment after his or her first episode. Subsequent exacerbations occur, leaving the patient unable to return fully to normal life.
- *Group 4* patient has persistent symptoms despite optimal treatment, and with increasingly higher levels of impairment following each relapse. Return to normality is rarely possible for these patients.

Another way to look at the same information is to examine outcome after 10 years and 30 years. What this tells is that things get better over time for many patients. As many as 25% of patients recover completely, about half of all patients do relatively well, some requiring more support than others; 10–15% of patients remain hospitalized or require substantial living support. The remaining small percentage of patients is deceased due to suicide or medical issues. The good news is that the average outcome for schizophrenia is much, much better than was previously believed.

PROGNOSTICATION

"Prognostication" is a technical term that means to forecast or predict. It refers to a *process* by which the clinician attempts to determine the future course of the illness in a specific patient. However, there are no certainties with prognostication, only educated guesses, based on research evidence and accumulated clinical tradition. Developing a prognosis is difficult during the first few days, weeks, or even months of the illness. It is only after gathering more specific information over time and taking into account well-known factors that allows clinicians to offer a more useful opinion about the future. We use the mnemonic PREDICT as a short-hand way of recalling the many factors that can influence the prognosis (Table 6.1).

Table **6.1** PREDICT Outcome

Prognostic Factor	Characteristics
Pre-diagnosis maladjustment	Patients who, even before the onset of psychotic symptoms, were already declining with regard to social, academic, and work functioning, and showing personality changes, tend to do worse over time. Having had no or minimal pre-diagnosis problems tends to have better outcomes.
Resource limitations	Access to healthcare is improving all the time, and it is important to maximize this opportunity. Not getting early and appropriate evaluation, not getting early and effective treatment, and following up with care are factors that can worsen outcome.
Early onset	Patients who develop schizophrenia earlier in life tend to have more negative outcomes than those who experience symptoms in their later years. On average, men experience an earlier onset of symptoms than women by a margin of five years. However, this is not set in stone, and for an individual patient, many factors unique to them will shape their long-term outcome.
Delay in treatment	When treatment is sought in the earliest stages of the disease, it is more likely to be successful than if there is significant delay. The longer the duration of untreated illness, worse the outcome. For this reason, it is very important to seek treatment as soon as you or a relative begins exhibiting the signs and symptoms of schizophrenia.
Inadequate treatment	Schizophrenia treatment may involve prescription medications, therapy, and other approaches. As different patients respond to different combinations of treatment approaches, it is unfortunately possible for patients to be undertreated, or to abandon the course of treatment if initial approaches are not successful. As a result, inadequate treatment is associated with a more negative course of the disease.

(Continued)

Table 6.1 (Continued)

Prognostic Factor	Characteristics
Cognitive impairment	Schizophrenia is associated with cognitive impairment (thinking difficulties), and greater the problems, poorer the outcome. If you or your relative has a known cognitive impairment, it is important to make your care team aware of this condition so that both may be considered and treated appropriately.
Treatment non-response	Patients who do not respond to initial rounds of treatment are more likely to experience worse outcomes. However, it is important to keep in mind that several treatment approaches (e.g., change of medication) may need to be tried before a successful course is found. If your first treatment attempt does not prove successful, do not give up hope. However, patients who do not respond to effective treatment within three years tend to do poorly. Regardless, it is important to talk to your care team about other treatment options that may be available.

Beyond those factors mentioned in Table 6.1, the following additional influences are known to have a positive or negative impact on the course of the disease and the success of its treatments (Table 6.2). Some of the prognostic elements are determined by nature, and are therefore unchangeable. However, there are other factors—called environmental factors—that can be modified.

Do keep in mind that *none of these factors* can definitively predict the course for any one individual with schizophrenia. Having more "negative" factors may suggest an unfavorable prognosis, but that is not a guarantee of a lower quality of life. In fact, it is possible that the overall prognosis may change over time as newer treatments become available.

Having more negative predictive factors may lead to an unfavorable prognosis, but that is not a guarantee of a lower quality of life.

Also, keep in mind that prognosis offered at this moment in time is based on information and circumstances that are current. Circumstances can change or new positive behaviors adopted by patients might improve the prognosis. For example, a homeless patient who now has all the support needed, including regular treatment, can dramatically and positively impact prognostication. On the other hand, repeatedly abusing drugs and skipping treatments can have the opposite effect.

Table 6.2 Additional Prognostic Factors

Favorable	Unfavorable
• Being female • The presence of obvious precipitating factors that contributed to disease onset • "Acute" (or fast) onset • Being married • Experiencing more positive than negative symptoms • Having good periods of recovery between schizophrenic episodes • Having a good support system	• Being male • "Insidious" (or slow) onset • The presence of neurological signs and symptoms • Having a history of perinatal trauma (e.g., maternal starvation or flu exposure) • Having a family history of schizophrenia • Having a personal history of violent behavior • Experiencing prominent negative symptoms • Having many relapses throughout the course of the illness

SUMMARY

- Prognostication is a process that attempts to determine the future course of the illness in a particular patient, based on what has been learned through years of observation and research on general patterns of schizophrenia progression.
- Having a prognosis—good or bad—is valuable for long-term lifestyle and treatment planning.
- Prognostication is a *process*: as more information becomes available with the passage of time, changes may be made to the initial prognosis.
- There are a variety of patient-related and treatment-related factors that play a role in prognostication; some are modifiable while others are not.
- A negative prognosis is not a guarantee that the patient will experience a very negative course of disease.

SECTION 3

Treatment

Medical Treatment of Schizophrenia
Common Medication Side Effects
Psychological and Rehabilitative Treatments
Treatment Nonadherence
Achieving Maximal Recovery

CHAPTER 7

Medical Treatment of Schizophrenia

If anything, the only periods when he (John Nash) was relatively free of hallucinations, delusions and the erosion of will
were the periods following either insulin treatment or the use
of antipsychotics.

SYLVIA NASAR, AUTHOR OF *A BEAUTIFUL MIND*

The aim of the medical treatment of schizophrenia is maximal recovery, which may include absence of all symptoms and complete return
to baseline functioning. However, there is a great deal of variability in
the level of recovery that is achieved by an individual patient. There are
many factors, specific to an individual, that will influence the degree of
recovery Regardless, a majority of patients will improve with medical
treatment, and many will achieve high levels of recovery.

Medical treatment for schizophrenia can be initiated, or restarted, in
several settings, but the principle for utilizing medications is the same in
all settings:

Emergency clinic
Inpatient service (during hospitalization)
Outpatient clinic
Mobile outreach service

GENERAL PRINCIPLES OF TREATMENT

Since schizophrenia is a lifelong disorder, your clinicians will begin by
assessing the specific phase of the illness course you are currently experiencing. In general, there are four phases of schizophrenic illness: the
prodromal phase, the psychotic phase (during which active symptoms

are present), convalescence (the recovery from symptomatic periods), and the stable phase (a time when symptoms are not present or unchanging).

Identifying these phases allows care teams to plan a multipronged approach to managing the illness and its consequences, and create a comprehensive plan for managing this illness. Treatment plans for each phase will probably involve a combination of pharmacotherapy ("brain-focused" treatment) and psychotherapy ("person-focused" treatment), as well as social and rehabilitative services.

Unfortunately, treatment phases do not always progress in a neat, straightforward fashion. The transition from one phase to the next tends to be fuzzy, which is why effective treatment plans involve different treatments and approaches.

Regardless of the patient's current phase of illness, his or her chances of a favorable outcome are improved if the following principles are established with the care team at the outset of treatment:

Early diagnosis and intervention. In recent years, there is an increasing emphasis on identifying and intervening early in the illness, that is, even before full-blown psychotic symptoms manifest. Many patients with schizophrenia show what is called *prodromal symptoms*, that is, mild positive and negative symptoms, social withdrawal, and functional decline beginning months, or even years before the first psychotic episode. It is now known that the longer such symptoms go untreated, the worse the outcome is likely to be. Follow-up studies show that about a third of such patients go on to develop psychotic disorders. While it is not clear that antipsychotic drugs (APDs) are the first line of treatment in such cases, studies suggest that psychotherapeutic treatments such as cognitive behavioral therapy can be very helpful.

Therapeutic alliance is a trusting and *collaborative* relationship between the patient and clinician. A strong therapeutic alliance provides a safe and forward-looking environment to tackle schizophrenia, and has been shown to positively influence outcome. Your care team should consistently operate from a therapeutic mind-set, which helps you or your relative to both identify and access any necessary treatment resources.

Collaboration is working *together* toward a goal. Rather than being a passive receiver of treatment, the patient should be a collaborating partner in his or her own treatment. Ideally, your clinician rather than "handing out" treatment should take a collaborative attitude and seek out feedback from you or your relative. A successful collaboration occurs when it is "we together" who will battle the illness, rather than "you" or "me."

Education about the illness and its treatment (also called psycho-education) is critical for both the patient and his or her support network. The better one is educated about the illness, the easier it is to understand why, for example, it is vital to take medications as prescribed and to keep up with follow-up appointments. Knowledge about the course of the illness can help identify early signs of relapse and provides strategies for managing side effects or persistent symptoms. Psychoeducation is a continuous process that extends throughout the different phases of the illness. Besides, there is always new scientific information emerging about schizophrenia that may improve treatments.

THE NEXT STEPS

Plans for managing the symptoms of schizophrenia typically follow a standardized process to ensure each patient's individual needs are met. The following is the general process clinicians, including us, use to develop an individualized treatment plan:

Consent. For legal and therapeutic reasons, patients must consent to their treatment, and they must be educated about the specifics of their treatment plans before they are undertaken (*informed consent*). Although the severity of a patient's symptoms may prevent him or her from consenting in full measure, the presence of psychosis doesn't necessarily interfere with the consenting process. You should know that you do have the legal right to refuse treatment, as long as you are not an imminent threat or legally considered incompetent. However, you would have to consider very carefully why you would refuse treatment that could vastly reduce the suffering from schizophrenia. It is also important to give consent to allow the care team to communicate with your family, so that they can share information that will assist in improving ongoing care.

Identify key symptoms. Typically, the most problematic behaviors are addressed first. Since antipsychotic medications have broad-ranging effects on reducing symptoms, improvements are also seen in other symptoms (sleep and appetite can normalize, energy improves, communication improves). It is important to recognize that different symptoms resolve over different time periods, therefore one shouldn't become impatient if all the problems are not resolved immediately. Your care team will discuss what the short-term and long-term treatment targets are.

Duration of initial medication trial. Once a medication is selected, most clinicians will recommend a treatment trial lasting at least 8–12 weeks. If, however, there are no benefits from the first medication trial, alert your doctors. Your care team may decide to change the treatment earlier, since uncontrolled psychosis runs a greater risk of becoming chronic. Sometimes patients or relatives complain about feeling like "guinea pigs" during the initial medication trials. It is understandable to feel this way while the clinician attempts to identify the right medication, one that is most effective and with the least side effects. There is a reason for this—unfortunately there is no way to know in advance which medication will be most effective or have the least side effects. Thus, a bit of a trial-and-error process is to be expected.

Anticipate and monitor side effects. Your care team should educate you on the common side effects associated with the chosen medication, as well as on strategies for dealing with them (discussed in greater detail in chapter 8). Many side effects are mild and temporary. If you are experiencing unpleasant side effects, let your doctors know promptly, as it may be possible to lower the medication dose or change it.

Medication compliance. As mentioned earlier, it is vital to take medications as prescribed. It is quite common for patients to go off their medication (known as *nonadherence*) and to experience relapse as a consequence. Expect that your clinicians will check in with you periodically to determine whether you are still taking your prescriptions and that this follow-up, while potentially annoying, is done out of concern for your health and well-being.

"Plan B." There is always an alternative if the current treatment is ineffective or the side effects are too troublesome. There is no "end of the line" when it comes to treatment options—there are different medications, different combinations, different therapy approaches.

A MEDICAL APPROACH TO MANAGING SYMPTOMS

The treatment of schizophrenia was transformed, over 60 years ago, with the use of a drug called chlorpromazine, the first effective pharmacological antipsychotic. Since then, numerous antipsychotic agents have come to market, giving care teams plenty of options to treat schizophrenia.

What Are Antipsychotic Agents?

Antipsychotic drugs are a group of medications that are used to treat psychotic disorders, such as schizophrenia. These drugs used to be referred to as major tranquilizers in the past, though you probably will not hear this term used very commonly.

Which Antipsychotic Drug Will I Receive?

Depending on your unique clinical situation, your care team may decide to offer one of the several available antipsychotic drugs—we will refer them to as APD. The choice to initiate a specific APD for you depends on a number of factors. For example, whether you need pill, liquid, or injectable form of the medicine may determine a specific APD. Other determining factors are whether you are on other medications (to avoid drug interactions) or have a medical condition that might be affected by the APD. Additionally, factors such as age, gender, family history, and previous treatments may be factored into the decision. One common reason that determines the choice of APD (and other medications) is whether your insurance covers the medication or is available in the hospital (known as formulary). Your psychiatrist will weigh in on all these aspects. Other medications, such as antianxiety medications, may be prescribed at the same time to manage other symptoms such as anxiety, agitation, and sleep problems.

Each APD has a *profile* that is based on the biological mechanisms that may underlie its effectiveness, its side effects, how long it stays in the body, and how the body breaks it down. This profile, while somewhat helpful in clinical decision making, is not helpful in matching a specific APD with a specific patient. In other words, we do not yet have a way to know which patient should get what drug.

Commonly Prescribed Antipsychotics

Over the past 60 years a large number of APDs have been introduced into treatment, most of which are still used. The first group of APDs is referred to as *first-generation* APDs. In recent years, a group of APDs—referred to as *second-generation* APDs—are now the most commonly used first-line treatments. Thus, a wide variety of APDs are available, and there is abundant experience in utilizing these for schizophrenia.

The list that follows is shown *alphabetically* by the chemical name, since trade names (name that a company gives a drug) differ across the world (Table 7.1). The trade names mentioned here apply to the United States.

Many APDs come in different forms, each of which is suited to different needs:

Tablets and capsules. These are the most common form of medication, though an occasional patient may have trouble with these preparations, such as trouble swallowing them. There are quick-dissolving tablets that can be helpful in such instances, but available for very few APDs.

Liquid preparations. Several APDs can be delivered as a liquid that can be mixed into juice (especially helpful for older adult and child patients), or those having trouble swallowing pills.

Rapid-acting injections. This formulation is typically used in a hospital setting for managing agitation or aggressive behaviors.

Table 7.1 Commonly Used Antipsychotic Drugs

	Chemical Name	Trade Name
First-Generation APDs	Chlorpromazine	Thorazine, Largactil
	Fluphenazine	Prolixin, Permitil
	Haloperidol	Haldol
	Loxapine	Loxitane
	Perphenazine	Trilafon
	Thiothixene	Navane
	Trifluoperazine	Stelazine
Second-Generation APDs	Aripiprazole	Abilify
	Asenapine	Saphris
	Clozapine	Clozaril
	Iloperidone	Fanapt
	Lurasidone	Latuda
	Olanzapine	Zyprexa
	Paliperidone	Invega
	Quetiapine	Seroquel
	Risperidone	Risperdal, Consta
	Ziprasidone	Geodon

Long-acting injectable (LAI) APD. Also known as *depot* medications, they are special injectable preparations that release medicine slowly into the body. They are as effective as oral APDs. LAIs are administered once or twice a month, and widely used when patients have difficulty taking oral medications reliably, or unable to follow up on a dependable basis. LAIs offer several advantages (fewer appointments, very few or no pills to swallow daily, no temptation to skipping pills).

Starting Antipsychotic Treatment

The two most common clinical situations in which APDs are started are new-onset psychosis and relapse following nonadherence. However, psychiatrists may switch APDs at any time during the course of the illness, either because of side effects or because of inadequate treatment response.

Starting an APD for *first-episode psychosis* requires careful assessment of symptoms, disease course, and concerns about specific side effects. In most cases, second-generation APDs are used. Since this may be the patient's first exposure to an APD, the general practice is to start with a low dose, and increase gradually. The *start low and go slow* approach minimizes the risk of side effects. The "final" dose depends on what is most effective with the least side effects. In general, patients starting with new treatment tend to have a very good response at relatively low doses. The research evidence, and our own studies, indicate a good treatment response in more than 70% of patients.

The other situation when APDs are started (or restarted) is when patients discontinue APDs for whatever reason and experience a relapse. If you or your relative goes off your established treatment regimen, your care team will need to know about your previous treatment history because an APD that was helpful in the past is very likely to work again.

How Long Will Treatments Last?

The aim of treatment is to reach maximal benefit using the lowest effective dose, while also minimizing any side effects. Since the *start low and go slow* approach is desired and generally the safest, it may take from a few days to weeks to reach the proper dosage.

Once the optimal dose is reached, and the patient is stable and doing well, a common question asked is about treatment duration. Research evidence suggests that treatment in most instances needs to be continued for life in order to *maintain* recovery from symptoms.

What to Do When Medication Doesn't Work

There is good reason to believe that treatment with APDs will help you or your relative experience significant symptom relief, especially when combined with the psychological and rehabilitative treatments, described in chapter 9. However, a significant number of patients show little improvement with initial trial of APDs. There are several options available that your care team may pursue:

Changing medications. As mentioned earlier, there is no way at present to predict which APD will be the most effective for you. Therefore, it is not uncommon to try several different APDs before pinpointing the one that works most effectively.

Combining medications. In some situations, for example, when symptoms are not responding to a single APD, a combination treatment may be required. While there are no APD combinations that are approved by the FDA for psychosis alone, research and clinical experience suggests that carefully planned APD combinations may offer benefits to some patients. That said, using two APDs might further increase the risk of side effects.

Exploring alternative medications. If APDs alone are not providing the level of symptom relief desired, your care team may look to other types of medication to treat specific symptoms or conditions that may occur alongside primary schizophrenia. When standard APDs are not effective, clozapine may be useful as the next step, though it has significant side effects as well. Your clinician may consider antidepressants, mood stabilizers, or antianxiety medications.

Electroconvulsive therapy (ECT). Despite the negative portrayals found in all forms of media, ECT today is administered in a humane way; it makes use of general anesthesia and muscle relaxants to minimize the risk of physical distress. By no means a common treatment for schizophrenia, ECT does offer an option for some patients whose schizophrenia is not well controlled by standard treatments.

Enrolling in drug trials. Another option for patients is the participation in approved drug trials. However, one has to carefully weigh the potential risks and benefits (the consenting process in research). Also, at the end of the research project, the experimental drug may no longer be available to you. Further, most well-designed treatment studies utilize a research approach called random-assignment double-blind, in which you have a 50–50 chance that you'll actually receive the drug and not a substance without any clinical effect.

As a reminder, most patients do very well with currently available treatments. Those who do less well still have many options available. Also, there are new treatments being developed all the time. It is important not to be discouraged and keep working with your care team to get the best treatment available.

OTHER PROBLEMS DURING A PSYCHOTIC EPISODE

Agitation. There are many reasons for someone to become agitated (disturbed). It could be due to the underlying symptoms associated with schizophrenia (e.g., paranoia can lead to aggressive behaviors), as well irritability, alcohol and drug intoxication, or withdrawal. Even some side effects, such as severe akathisia (APD-related restlessness), can lead to agitation. If you are in a very agitated state, and are able to communicate this distress, you will be assisted by clinicians to find a quiet space. If that's still not helpful, you'll be offered medications (APDs or antianxiety agents) that will provide quick relief. If you are extremely agitated that you may be a danger to yourself or others, obviously your safety and those around you is paramount. Frequently, in such situations, clinicians will use injectable form of APDs or antianxiety agents to rapidly decrease an agitation.

Insomnia. Many patients experience sleep disruptions, related to either the disease itself or to prescribed medications. Insomnia (sleeplessness) is common during the active phase of symptoms. Lack of sleep can contribute to irritability, even agitation, and worsen psychosis. When APDs are initiated, the overall positive effect can also improve sleep. Some APDs have sleepiness (sedation) as side effect, which can be a temporary advantage. However, if insomnia persists, there are medications that can be used on a short-term basis called hypnotics. Because of their addictive potential, these medications are used for short periods of time. If insomnia becomes long-standing or is not responding to short-term treatments, then it may require a referral to a sleep evaluation clinic.

SUMMARY

- The medical treatment of schizophrenia has been in existence for over sixty years.
- The specific treatment approach depends on whether you or your relative are in a prodromal phase, active psychotic phase, convalescence, or the stable phase.
- Treatment success also depends on working effectively with your care team that requires therapeutic alliance, proper collaboration, and ongoing education, regardless of the current illness phase.
- Clinicians follow established procedures when initiating the medical treatment of schizophrenia, which generally includes obtaining consent, securing medical clearance, identifying target symptoms, planning the duration of a medication trial, anticipating and monitoring side effects, monitoring for compliance and coming up with alternate treatment strategies. Understanding your doctors' management plans makes the treatment process go more smoothly for all involved.
- Antipsychotic drugs (APDs) produce symptom relief in roughly 70% of patients. APDs can be divided into two classes: first-generation APDs (which were introduced in the 1950s, but are still used), and second-generation APDs (introduced in 1990s) that now are usual first-line treatments.
- Choosing the appropriate APD involves taking into account a variety of factors, such as age, past treatment history, risk of side effects, coexisting medical conditions, route of delivery (as in, pills versus injections), and insurance coverage.
- There is no research data to suggest that one APD is more effective than another, but different medications seem to work better for some patients than for others.
- If the initial APD trial proves ineffective, there are many options.
- Current research suggests that most patients require lifelong treatment. This is not a certainty. However, stopping medication without supervision is highly risky, because relapse is very probable.

CHAPTER 8

Common Medication Side Effects

That by applying a remedy to one sore, you will provoke another;
and that which removes the one ill symptom produces others.
SIR THOMAS MORE (1478–1535)

Antipsychotic medications are highly effective for the treatment of psychosis symptoms, but unfortunately can have troublesome side effects. Fortunately, the majority of side effects can be avoided by the appropriate choice of the medication, adjusting doses, and/or using alternative or adjunct medications.

Since persistent side effects are the most common reason to stop treatment, it is in your best interest to be aware of these common medication side effects. Effective management of side effects starts by recognitioning, and alerting your care team for proper interventions.

ABNORMAL MOVEMENTS

There are varieties of movement problems (known as *movement disorders*) that may occur at the beginning of APD treatment, or in some cases follow a long period of treatment. Management of movement disorders may involve lowering the APD dose, changing the APD, or using medication that counters the side effect. Some of these movement disorders are:

> Akathisia (a-ka-thees-ia). This is the experience of jitteriness or restlessness, primarily in the legs. There is increased fidgetiness, and sometimes it is difficult to sit still; pacing is common. It typically starts as soon as 2 weeks, and as long as 10 weeks, after starting the APD. However, the possibility of developing akathisia is much

lower with second generation APDs compared to first generation APDs. When akathisia presents, the usual approach to managing it is to lower the APD dose or change the APD.

Parkinsonism. The name derives from the fact that the symptoms of this side effect mirror, but are not the same as, true Parkinson's disease. Patients may experience tremors (usually of the hands), stiffness, slow movements, and shuffling gait. As with akathisia, the risk of Parkinsonism is much lower with second-generation APDs. Treatment is straightforward—reducing the APD, adding an *anticholinergic* agent, or switching the APD.

Tardive dyskinesia. This side effect is different from other movement disorders in that it tends to appear after long-term treatment with APDs. Tardive dyskinesia (commonly referred to as TD) can involve any part of the body, but most frequently is seen in hands, face, jaw, mouth, and tongue. The movements are described as jerky or slow and writhing, or a combination. Some patients are unaware that they have TD, and only when others observe it will it be identified. The risk of developing TD is lower with second-generation APDs (3.9% new cases annually) compared to first-generation APDs (5.5% new cases annually). Older persons and those with medical conditions, such as diabetes, are at higher risk. Because this side effect may be permanent in a small number of patients, care teams are vigilant about signs of TD, and perform regular assessments to detect it. There is no definitive cure. However, a number of management strategies are used, including dose adjustment, changing APDs, and using other medications, that have been found helpful.

Dystonia. Dystonia is a painful muscular spasm in any part of the body, but commonly involving the neck, jaw, tongue, or eyes. The majority of cases present within four days after starting an APD, primarily first-generation APDs such as haloperidol and fluphenazine. Dystonia is uncommon with second-generation APDs. Young males appear to be at somewhat a higher risk of this side effect. Treatment with anticholinergic medications is very effective.

METABOLIC SYNDROME

This term—"metabolic syndrome"—may not be familiar to you, but it is an important issue in relation to APD treatment because this condition increases the risk of diabetes, heart disease, stroke, and related problems. The medical definition of metabolic syndrome that is most widely accepted is the presence of *three or more* of the following conditions:

- A waist circumference (girth) greater than 40' in men and 35' in women
- Fasting blood triglycerides (type of fat) greater than 150 mg/dl
- Blood HDL ("good") cholesterol less than 40 mg/dl in men and 50 mg/dl in women
- Blood pressure greater than 130/85 mmHg
- Fasting glucose levels greater than 110 mg/dl

Certain APDs have a greater risk of causing the metabolic syndrome, such as clozapine and olanzapine. However, there are other influences that play a role as well—genetic factors, being obese, and physically inactive before start of treatment.

Your physician will determine whether you have the metabolic syndrome or are at risk. If diagnosed, you may be advised to improve your diet and increase physical activity. Additionally, the APD may be switched, or medications that specifically address elevated blood pressure or increased lipids (fats) in the blood may be offered.

WEIGHT GAIN

Although excess weight and obesity are a problem for modern societies everywhere, the seriousness of the issue is magnified in the case of schizophrenia. Weight gain in patients may be associated with preexisting metabolic syndrome, or as a consequence of lifestyle changes following the diagnosis of schizophrenia, or after APD initiation. When weight gain reaches a certain level, it is called obesity. The currently accepted measure of body weight is body mass index (*BMI*), which is calculated using a very specific formula (see Glossary). The resulting numbers are categorized as shown in Table 8.1:

Table 8.1 The Ranges of Body Mass Index (BMI)

BMI	Weight Status
Below 18.5	Underweight
18.5–24.9	Normal
25.0–29.9	Overweight
30.0 and Above	Obese

Weight gain associated with APDs usually results from increased appetite and the excessive food consumption that follows. The risk of weight gain due to specific APDs varies. The greatest risk lies with clozapine and least for ziprasidone; other APDs have a wide range of risk for weight gain. Typically, the weight gain is maximal during the early period of treatment, and appears to level off with long-term treatment.

Strategies for managing weight gain are straightforward in principle (switching APD, weight loss program, lifestyle changes), but in reality, challenging to follow through. This is because of the inactive lifestyle and unhealthy dietary habits, combined with symptoms of schizophrenia, particularly negative symptoms, that add to the burden.

However, weight gain is a very serious issue that requires vigilance and active intervention. Adding to the burden of weight gain on health is cigarette smoking, which occurs at very high rates (50%), and adds to the medical complications related to excess weight. Therefore, every effort should be made by patients and caregivers to incorporate a healthy lifestyle from the very beginning because patients with schizophrenia have a higher death rate, at an earlier age, primarily do to cardiovascular disease.

DIABETES

The concern about diabetes (previously called adult onset diabetes and now referred to as type II) exists with any APD associated with weight gain. Other factors that add to the risk are family history of diabetes, having diabetes during pregnancy, high blood pressure, being older than 45 years, and certain ethnic groups (African, Hispanic, Asian).

Your care team may test your fasting blood sugar level regularly to detect the presence of diabetes before it can lead to health complications. Once diabetes is diagnosed (or preexisting diabetes worsens), patients should follow standard diabetes treatment guidelines, while switching to an APD that is less likely to contribute to diabetes, if clinically possible.

COMPREHENSIVE LIST OF APD SIDE EFFECTS

Table 8.2 (listed *alphabetically*, not in order of importance) is provided as a general overview of other APD-related side effects that you may hear about or experience. Note, though, that the vast majority of side effects are not severe and are short-lived. While severe side effects can occur, as with any medication, they are very rare. Your care team will be vigilant about serious side effects.

Table 8.2 Common APD-Related Side Effects

Side Effect	Technical Term	Solution
Blurred vision		The most common reason for blurred vision is the effect some APDs have on the neurotransmitter *acetylcholine*. If these APDs can't be avoided, therapeutic drugs that treat the side effects (e.g., pilocarpine or bethanecol) may be used.
Cholesterol increase	Hypercholesterolemia	Elevations in triglyceride and cholesterol levels occur with atypical APDs, particularly clozapine and olanzapine, but are not always linked with weight gain. Switching to another APD may halt or reverse this. Conservative weight loss measures including diet changes and exercise plans should be initiated. Lipid-lowering agents may be prescribed.
Constipation		Constipation is a common problem due to APDs, low fiber intake, and immobility. It can be treated with increased fiber intake (through bran, vegetables and fruits, or psyllium husk), prunes, increased non-calorie fluid intake, stool softeners (e.g., docusate), and exercise. Laxatives should be used sparingly to prevent dehydration and dependence.
Decrease in white blood cells	Leukopenia	Leukopenia is determined by laboratory blood testing. When it occurs in schizophrenia, it is usually temporary, but should be watched carefully, as it can be a sign of more serious conditions like agranulocytosis, that is seen primarily with clozapine treatment.

(Continued)

Table 8.2 (Continued)

Side Effect	Technical Term	Solution
Drooling or excessive saliva	Sialorrhea	Sialorrhea is common with clozapine treatment and does not go away with time. Placing a towel over the pillow can minimize the discomfort at night (when this side effect tends to worsen), as can treatment with supportive anticholinergic agents.
Dry mouth	Xerostomia	Dry mouth is caused by the same "anticholinergic" (impacting acetylcholine levels) effect as blurred vision and constipation. Chewing sugar-free gum, sipping cold, calorie-free fluids or sucking on ice chips may be helpful. A pilocarpine rinse may also be indicated for severe cases.
Electrocardiogram (EKG) changes	Q-Tc prolongation refers to a specific change observed on an EKG that reflects changes in the heart rhythm	Q-Tc prolongation is infrequent, but when present increases the risk of sudden death. Patients with a history of heart disease should be closely monitored, and be treated with APDs that are less likely to cause this side effect.
Emotional discomfort or a feeling of unease	Dysphoria	Dysphoria can be a consequence of treatment, though many patients find it difficult to describe it, and can therefore be easily overlooked, or is mistakenly attributed to the illness. Changes in treatment on the basis of this side effect should be made cautiously, as dysphoria can be a symptom of schizophrenia. However, a trial lowering of the dose or a switching of APDs may be worthwhile.

Side Effect	Technical Term	Solution
Erection problems	Erectile dysfunction	Lowering the dose or changing the APD can be helpful. Treatment with sildenafil has also been used successfully in cases of antidepressant-induced erectile dysfunction. As with any drug treatment, there are side effects of sildenafil, so using it should be under supervision.
Faintness or lightheadedness	Orthostatic hypotension (A fall in blood pressure that occurs when arising from a seated or lying down position)	This side effect tends to occur early in treatment, generally temporary lasting no more than 4–6 weeks. If you find yourself feeling faint when getting up, stand up slowly (or get out of bed slowly), elevate your headrest, and increase your fluids and salt intake. If this side effect persists, speak with your care team, who may prescribe fludrocortisone to help manage the symptom.
Heartbeat increased over 100 beats/ minute	Tachycardia	Tachycardia tends to be a temporary side effect seen with certain APDs or in patients experiencing orthostatic hypotension. Your care team may treat this side effect with atenolol if it persists.
Missed periods	Hyperprolactinemia (Chronic prolactin elevation may cause breast leakage, the development of excess breast tissue, and possible loss of bone density)	This problem is less common with second-generation APDs, but not totally absent. Switching APDs with less likelihood of prolactin increase is the usual solution.
Muscle rigidity	(a) Neuroleptic malignant syndrome (NMS) (b) Dystonia	(a) NMS is very rare, but it is a *medical emergency* because it is potentially fatal. It can occur with all APDs. MS is

(*Continued*)

Table 8.2 (Continued)

Side Effect	Technical Term	Solution
		the sudden onset of muscle rigidity, high fever, with changes in consciousness (agitation, stupor), unstable blood pressure, sweating, and excessive salivation. If you suspect NMS, contact your care team immediately or 9-1-1. (b) See dystonia description earlier.
Orgasm problems	Anorgasmia	Although a sensitive topic, it is important to alert your care team. Too often patients stop the APD instead of discussing this issue. Lowering the dose or changing the APD can be helpful. More specific treatment may be offered.
Seizures		Seizures usually occur with rapid increases in APD dose (or with specific doses of clozapine). Dividing up doses may help control this side effect, while anticonvulsant treatment may be needed in other cases.
Sex drive decrease	Decreased libido	Decreased libido occurs in roughly 25–50% of patients and can be reversed by switching APDs.
Sleepiness or tiredness	Sedation	In most instances, sedation is a temporary side effect that lasts no more than two weeks. If it interferes with your functioning, talk to your care team about changing your dosing schedule to bedtime, reducing your daytime dosing, or switching to a less sedating APD.

Side Effect	Technical Term	Solution
Temperature increase	Hyperthermia	Drugs known as antipyretics can be used to treat the mild elevation of body temperature that is common during initial treatment (particularly with clozapine). Persistent hyperthermia or higher average body temperatures can be indicative of serious conditions and should be promptly investigated.

SUMMARY

- A variety of side effects can occur with APD treatment; fortunately most are temporary and not very troublesome.
- Early detection and proper management of side effects is critically important to prevent distress, avoid treatment nonadherence, and subsequent relapse.
- Abnormal body movements (movement disorders) such as akathisia, Parkinsonism, and dystonia are generally seen early in the course of treatment, and effective treatments are available. Tardive dyskinesia (TD) presents after long-term treatment. Since there is no standard treatment for TD, regular monitoring is necessary. Switching APDs with less risk for TD is part of the management approach.
- Patients with schizophrenia appear to be at a higher risk for developing metabolic syndrome, a cluster of conditions that can lead to type II diabetes, coronary heart disease, stroke, and peripheral vascular disease. Treatment for this side effect may include switching antipsychotics and adopting healthier lifestyle habits.
- Weight gain is relatively common, particularly with clozapine or olanzapine. If weight gain is detected, which is usually early in treatment, management includes adopting a healthy lifestyle, and when practical, changing the APD to one with less weight gain risk.
- Patients with schizophrenia have twice the occurrence rates of diabetes than the general population. Consequently, your care team will closely monitor your blood sugar levels after initiating APD treatment.
- There are potentially deadly side effects associated with APDs, such as neuroleptic malignant syndrome. Fortunately, it is very rare. Know what signs and symptoms to watch out for, and consult with your clinician immediately or call 9-1-1.

CHAPTER 9

Psychological and Rehabilitative Treatments

It is better for us to see the destination we wish to reach, than the point of departure.

JULES VERNE, FRENCH NOVELIST

Despite the generally effective treatment of schizophrenia, attaining psychological wellness and reintegration into society can be challenging. While APDs are largely effective in controlling the severity of positive symptoms, many patients continue to experience some degree of disability. The reasons for such disability include persistent positive and negative symptoms, and thought disturbance. Additionally, diminished social skills, dependency, poor job prospects, stigma, and isolation contribute to this burden. Therefore, a comprehensive approach to addressing psychosocial and rehabilitative recovery is critically important.

It is no longer the case that psychosocial treatments and rehabilitation are an afterthought. From the outset, the care team will be devising a comprehensive plan that may include individual, group, and community-based psychosocial therapies. One of the great advantages of psychosocial treatments is the general absence of side effects!

PSYCHOLOGICAL TREATMENTS

The main forms of psychological interventions used with patients with schizophrenia are:

- Supportive psychotherapy
- Psychoeducation
- Cognitive behavioral therapy

- Cognitive enhancement therapy
- Metacognitive and mindfulness-based therapies

Supportive Psychotherapy

Supportive therapy (ST) offers patients a place to safely voice their concerns, and provides reassurance and encouragement, practical guidance on day-to-day matters, explanations, and clarifications. ST focuses less on specific symptoms or the underlying cognitive or emotional impairments; rather, it assists with coping, improving quality of life and self-esteem. ST is highly flexible in that it addresses patients' immediate concerns, whatever they may be, rather than a goal-oriented therapy. Thus, it is highly valuable and is a useful adjunct to other forms of therapy.

Psychoeducation

While psychoeducation is not a classical form of therapy, its underlying principles result in improved awareness, improved treatment adherence, better coping stills, and better informed family and caregivers, which in turn improves empathy and decreases hostility. There are many important reasons, established by good research, to participate in a psychoeducation program—reduced relapse rates, better symptom control, as well as better psychosocial and family functioning. To be maximally beneficial, psychoeducation should be revisited as many times as necessary.

There are many variants of the psychoeducation programs, but each has a central goal—to assist in achieving maximal recovery (Table 9.1). We outline components of psychoeducation that has the mnemonic CARE LIST (Table 9.1), which is a list of common principles (not in order of importance):

Cognitive Behavioral Therapy (CBT)

CBT is a form of therapy that is action-oriented, in which the therapist helps the patient change problem behaviors by modifying the underlying negative or distorted thinking. It has been widely used for depression, anxiety disorders, and personality disorders. Although in recent years CBT has been found also to be effective for schizophrenia, it is also not commonly used. Inquire with your care team about its availability in your area.

Table 9.1 Psychoeducation Principles (CARE LIST)

Key Issue	Where to Find More Information
Coping skills	Chapter 15
Alliances and supports	Chapters 13–15, Appendix C
Relapse prevention tips: the four Ss	Chapter 11
Early warning signs	Appendix D
Lifestyle issues (diet, sleep and exercise, substance use)	Chapters 11, 15; Appendix D
Illness: Diagnosis, causes, meanings of terms	Chapters 2–6, 17–18; Glossary
Strengths	Appendix D
Treatments (medications, side effects, other treatments, emergency contact information)	Chapters 7–11; Appendixes A and D

CBT is particularly effective in reducing the psychological effects of persistent positive symptoms in chronic patients, and may even speed up recovery in acutely ill patients. The reason CBT is thought to help symptoms such as delusions and hallucinations is because they are believed to stem from a tendency to overestimate coincidences, jump to conclusions, assume that internal experiences come from external sources, and blame others when things are not going well (known as *information-processing bias*).

Some terms you will hear used in CBT:
Automatic thoughts are those that come to mind immediately, without effort, when a particular situation occurs. These automatic thoughts result in a *reaction* to the situation, leading to problem behaviors. For example, if you find someone casually looking at you, your automatic thought might be that he or she is snooping, and you might get angry. CBT involves challenging these automatic thoughts.

Cognitive restructuring is about identifying and adjusting incorrect thought patterns (*schemas*), replacing them with positive thoughts and beliefs.

Relaxation techniques are a variety of methods or approaches to help relieve emotional and physical stress. Common techniques include muscle relaxation, meditation, and exercise.

Table 9.2 ABC Model of CBT Table

Activating event	Something that sets off a chain of thoughts and behaviors; also called *trigger*
Beliefs	Automatic thoughts that occur when the activating event happens
Consequences	How you feel and behave when you have those beliefs

The CBT process:

Assessment and engagement. This is the first phase, in which there is education about the process, and history is reviewed. Thoughts and feelings, as well as understanding of ongoing experiences, are explored.

Behavior change. The next stage is to begin making connections between A-B-C, and begin to explore how automatic thoughts are not necessarily based in reality; by recognizing this, behavior changes for the better.

Consolidation. Once the skill is learned, and the more it is practiced (by doing homework and trying it out in real life), the easier it becomes to avoid jumping to conclusions.

Cognitive Enhancement Therapy

A substantial number of schizophrenia patients have impairments in cognition, in areas such as psychomotor speed, attention, working memory (immediate memory) and executive function (planning), verbal learning, and social cognition. These problems strongly predict functional outcome. "Cognitive remediation" (a term we dislike), training, or enhancement approaches involve either compensating for deficits (strategies to organize information, or other tools such as reminders, prompts, etc.) or approaches to restore cognitive functions based on learning specific techniques. Cognitive Adaptation Training is a set of techniques that help reduce the demand for complex thinking by creating checklists, reminders etc. The two primary approaches to improving thinking are the *drill-and-practice methods* and the *strategic methods*. The drill-and-practice approach focuses on repeating a thinking exercise until a useful level of skill is attained. Strategic approaches focus on developing tactics that aid in becoming more efficient in thinking and memory (e.g., remembering information in meaningful ways or using mnemonic procedures). The research evidence indicates that cognitive training can indeed improve cognition in schizophrenia, along with benefits to symptoms and daily functioning. However, overall strategic training (e.g., supported employment) provides stronger benefits. One comprehensive approach is cognitive enhancement therapy (CET) which combines these approaches, developed by Gerard Hogarty, Matcheri Keshavan, Shaun Eack, and colleagues in Pittsburgh.

Metacognitive and Mindfulness-Based Therapies

Metacognition refers to the ability to reflect about one's own thinking. Metacognitive therapy (MCT) is similar to CBT in terms of goals and some of the methods. While CBT focuses on "what" a person thinks, MCT targets "how" a person thinks.

At the heart of MCT is the idea that the content of the thoughts is not what matters most, but the *reaction* to those thoughts. Early research has shown that MCT reduces distress associated with delusions. Additional benefits include certain types of memory, and satisfaction with relationships. While availability of MCT is limited, its use in schizophrenia shows significant promise. Check with your care team whether they offer MCT.

Mindfulness-based therapies focus on reducing perseveration (repetitive thinking) about negative and stressful events. It works by:

- Allowing such negative events to come into *clear focus*
- Accepting the thoughts about these events with *no judgment*
- Then letting the thoughts and feelings *pass naturally*

Another approach, *acceptance and commitment therapy*, utilizes meditation and related exercises to help individuals experience depth and accept symptoms such as psychosis in a nonjudgmental manner. A recent book by Dr. Nicola Wright and her colleagues discusses this approach in great detail (see Appendix C for details).

Social Skills Training

Verbal and nonverbal skills are required for all socialization. Patients with schizophrenia can have problems in a variety of social skills, such as making eye contact during a conversation, listening attentively, expressing interest in the conversation, or even having the ability to hold a conversation. These challenges can develop before the onset of illness, and continue even after effective control of positive symptoms.

The underlying cause may include the positive and negative symptoms, as well as cognitive deficits.

Social skills training (SST) helps patients learn to recognize social signals, in order to learn how to act appropriately with other people. SST involves practicing selected behaviors in individual or group therapy. SST can also be used in order to improve job-specific social skills, thus improving the prospects of obtaining and keeping a job. SST is valuable in enhancing the capacity for independent living.

REHABILITATION

Rehabilitation (from Latin *habilitas*, "to make able")—a collection of activities that address a broad variety of patient needs—is essential for *reintegration* back into the community. Since medical and psychological treatments are not solely effective means to restoring previous level of functioning, rehabilitation is a process by which recovery and quality of life can be improved. Rehabilitation includes case management, assertive community treatment (ACT), family interventions, supported employment, supported housing, and social skills training.

Here we address some elements of rehabilitation, while the rest of the topics are addressed in chapter 15 (Common Problems in Facing Schizophrenia).

Case Management

Case management refers to a collaborative process of assessment, planning, facilitation, care coordination, evaluation, and advocacy for options and services to meet an individual's and family's comprehensive health needs (The Case Management Society of America). Getting treatment can be confusing to coordinate due to numerous factors—visits for follow-up care, getting medications, attending groups and rehabilitation activities, arranging transportation for these visits, and so forth. Because these diverse, but necessary, tasks can be overwhelming to some patients, there is the risk of not utilizing these important treatment activities, leading to worsening health or relapse.

Intensive case management (ICM), a variation of case management, is useful for patients with greater needs. They also serve as links between inpatient and outpatient care, including discharge planning and connections to community programs.

Assertive Community Treatment

Assertive community treatment (ACT) is a comprehensive and coordinated set of services that aims to keep patients functioning well in the community, in order to minimize the need for hospitalization. ACT professionals provide a broad set of medical, psychiatric, and social services to patients in the community. They utilize mobile outreach clinical teams to reach patients who are unable or unwilling to come in for routine outpatient follow-ups.

SUMMARY

- Although APDs are quite effective in controlling the severity of most symptoms, many patients continue to have some degree of disability. In order to return the patient to the highest level of functioning and reintegration into the community, comprehensive psychosocial and rehabilitative treatments are important.
- The main forms of psychosocial interventions are supportive therapy, psychoeducation, cognitive behavioral therapy (CBT), cognitive enhancement therapy, social skills training, and newer approaches such as metacognitive therapy and mindfulness-based therapy.
- Psychoeducation is an important tool in facilitating insight about schizophrenia, consequently improving treatment adherence and outcomes.
- Cognitive behavioral therapy (CBT) is a form of action-oriented therapy in which the therapist helps the patient change problem behaviors by modifying the underlying negative or distorted thinking.
- Cognitive training approaches, such as cognitive enhancement therapy, help patients to recover from impaired thinking and improve real-world functioning.
- A third of patients experience persistent hallucinations and delusions that can be improved by utilizing a combination of these techniques.
- Social skills training (SST) helps patients re-acquire complex social skills, such as making friends, using a variety of techniques, such as instruction, modeling, feedback, and homework.
- Rehabilitation is a collection of activities that address a broad variety of patient needs that is essential for *reintegrating* back into the community.
- Case management is a program to help patients with practical matters, such as arranging for follow-up visits and transportation.
- Assertive community treatment (ACT) is a more intensive form of rehabilitative service with the goal of keeping patients out of the hospital.

CHAPTER 10

Treatment Nonadherence

Compliance is a major problem. Patients believe that once they're better, they no longer need the medication. It doesn't work that way.

KAY REDFIELD JAMISON, PH.D., AUTHOR OF *AN UNQUIET MIND*

Arguably, one of the greatest challenges in the management of schizophrenia is the issue of not taking medications. Adherence and compliance are other terms that are used interchangeably to mean following a prescribed regimen, and nonadherence and noncompliance mean the opposite.

There are many reasons why patients with schizophrenia fail to adhere to treatment or follow precise recommendations. In fact, as many as 75% of patients go on to become nonadherent within two years following their initial discharge. Independent of the reasons, nonadherence can be devastating for both patients and their families.

However, this issue is by no means unique to schizophrenia. Large-scale studies have found that people rarely take prescription drugs properly. For example, patients with diabetes average only a 20% adherence rate, despite facing nerve damage, kidney failure, heart disease, and other complications if diabetes is improperly treated. Even if nonadherence is a universal problem, schizophrenia may bring on additional challenges because of the nature of the disease, such as a lack of awareness of illness.

WHY TREATMENT NONADHERENCE OCCURS

Treatment nonadherence is *not* a personal failing! Of course, it can be frustrating to families and care teams when patients appear to be acting

Figure 10.1 Reasons for Treatment Nonadherence

against their own self-interest. However, being aware of the many reasons that lead to nonadherence may permit early identification of these problems, and these can be addressed proactively. Common reasons for treatment nonadherence are given in Figure 10.1.

TREATMENTS PRODUCE UNDESIRABLE SIDE EFFECTS

This is one of the most common reasons for nonadherence. As we discussed earlier, APDs and other types of medications can have side effects ranging from minor inconveniences to serious health concerns. Not being prepared (through education) about the nature of side effects, that they are usually not serious and temporary, can lead to unnecessary fears, and subsequent nonadherence. There can be sexual side effects that patients are reluctant to bring up because of their sensitive nature, and consequently stop treatment.

Therefore, if you or your relative are experiencing side effects, bring them to the attention of the care team. Do not go off medications, unless it is an emergency! They will be able to effectively address these concerns.

SOME PATIENTS ARE UNAWARE OF THEIR ILLNESS

Another important cause of nonadherence is being unaware of the illness (also referred to as poor insight or *anosognosia*). This is not the same thing as denial (rejection) of illness. It may be difficult to comprehend how someone could be unaware of the apparently obvious signs and symptoms of schizophrenia. But, prior to treatment, roughly half of all patients with schizophrenia are unaware that they're ill. The underlying mechanism for this unawareness is poorly understood, but it is seen in other neurological conditions, and presumed to be a form of brain dysfunction. However, illness unawareness is not a fixed symptom. It varies over time, and can improve with treatment.

MEDICATIONS MAY NOT BE WORKING

Antipsychotic and other medications are not equally effective in improving symptoms for everyone. Often, patients do not take the medications simply because they are not working. In such situations, make sure that you or your relative address this concern with your doctor. Your care team will also be monitoring this issue. Dose adjustments may be made, or alternative APDs may be prescribed.

COMPLEX TREATMENT SCHEDULES

In some instances, treatment can include multiple medications that have complicated schedules, which can lead to confusion. This causes medicine to be ingested incorrectly, resulting in taking too little medication or taking too much! Your doctor will attempt to simplify the regimen as much as possible, but at times, because of the nature of the medications, there are limitations as to how much simpler it can be made. If you live alone, you need to set up a system that works for you. Written schedules, pillboxes, reminder systems (smart caps, apps) can be invaluable. Family members, caregivers, or support staff can also check in periodically to ensure medication schedules are being followed.

MEDICATION AND TREATMENT COSTS ARE TOO HIGH

Patients on a limited or fixed income, as well as those with insufficient insurance coverage for medications, may be forced to make difficult decisions. Do I buy groceries this month or fill my prescriptions? Do I skip a recommended doctor visit because I've exceeded the limitations of my coverage and would be forced to pay the entire cost out of pocket? I can't afford the co-pay! I do not have travel money!

Unfortunately, some patients in this situation end up rationing their medication, perhaps by taking a pill every other day or by splitting pills in half to make them last longer. This tinkering has obvious negative effects on the patient's treatment. If you find yourself in this situation, talk to your care team about the different options that are available to you. Your doctor may be able to switch you to a cheaper generic version of your current medication, or switch to one that's covered under your insurer's formulary. Many medication manufacturers have programs to assist patients with no or low income. Your care team can assist you with applying for these programs.

STIGMA SURROUNDING TREATMENT

Having to take medications can be an uncomfortable reminder that one has an illness, made even more painful by the notion that treatment may be lifelong. The fear that this fact (having an illness) may become public knowledge, even among friends and extended family, can discourage patients from wanting to stay involved in treatment. A further fear is that "visible" medication side effects may disclose the fact that they suffer from a "mental" disorder. It is important to be able to discuss these fears openly, educate yourself about the treatment of schizophrenia, and carefully think about the tremendous risks of not staying in treatment.

MAXIMIZING ADHERENCE

Identifying risk factors for nonadherence that are *unique to your or your relative's situation* is the first step in prevention. There may be simple solutions, such as using pillboxes, or solutions that require more effort, such as switching medications to avoid side effects. The essential point is that there are solutions, and that you are not alone in dealing with this dilemma!

Be proactive about managing side effects. Given the possibility of medication side effects and its impact on treatment adherence, it is important to address any such symptoms before they can disrupt adherence. Speak to your doctor about dose adjustment, alternative medications (including monthly or biweekly injectable medications), or strategies for managing side effects, should they happen.

If the medication is not effective, alert your care team. If the current treatment is not providing good or satisfactory results, let your care team know. They may be focusing on symptoms that may seem important to address, but you may have a different set of concerns for which you want effective treatment.

Establish daily routines around taking medications. Regular daily routines (habits) increase the chances of successfully staying on medications and taking them correctly. Routines also reduce day-to-day stresses, for example, taking medication around the time of brushing teeth in the morning (and keeping the pill box near the tooth brush), or when entering the kitchen to prepare a meal. As we like to say—just be a "regular" person!

Refill prescriptions in a timely manner. Similar to taking medication on a schedule, picking up refills should also be done on a schedule. Many clinics have pharmacies attached to them, permitting a regular one-stop visit for clinic and medication pickup. Many pharmacies now send telephone, e-mail, or text message reminders well in advance of the refill date. Therefore, there is no real justification for forgetting to refill prescriptions on time.

Be watchful as recovery becomes apparent. Paradoxically, stopping medications may follow the experience of feeling better after treatment. This is true not just for APDs and schizophrenia, but also for many types of medications, such as antibiotics. It is important to remember that improvement is directly *due* to treatment, and stopping medications at this point is a setup for relapse (and the cycle of starting and stopping APDs starts over).

Use rewards. For you or your relative, setting up goals, with a reward when you reach these goals, can be a useful strategy! The rewards should not be bribes! The patient himself or herself, or caregiver and the patient jointly, can decide on reasonable rewards (preferably not too much candy!).

Talk to your doctor about injectable APDs. Some APDs are available as injections administered once in two or four weeks. These include haloperidol, risperidone, paliperidone, olanzapine, and aripiprazole, and can be very helpful to address the problem of nonadherence.

Compliance therapy. This method is based on brief *motivational interviewing* and cognitive therapy techniques, the goal of which are to increase patient awareness of the problems and consequences of nonadherence. Using the patient's own beliefs about his or her issues with treatment, a connection is made between these beliefs, nonadherence, and consequences, consequently increasing motivation to stay in treatment. Compliance therapy has shown improvements in the patients' attitude toward medications, insight, and treatment adherence. Find out whether compliance therapy is available in your area; it is not yet a routine treatment approach.

SUMMARY

- Nonadherence is the failure to follow prescribed treatment plans. Roughly three-quarters of patients with schizophrenia become nonadherent within two years of their initial discharge. This significantly increases the risk of relapse.
- Patients may become nonadherent for a variety of reasons—side effects, unawareness of their illness, frustration with lack of improvement, complicated treatment schedules, inability to afford treatment, or stigma.
- It is especially common for patients with schizophrenia who are responding well to treatment to believe that they no longer need to take prescribed medications.
- A variety of strategies can be used to minimize the risk of nonadherence, such as using written schedules, pill boxes, or linking medications with daily routine tasks. Injectable long-acting APDs can be very helpful.
- Treatment nonadherence is not a failing on the part of the patient. Creating a supportive environment that rewards adherence often produces better outcomes.

CHAPTER 11

Achieving Maximal Recovery

Healing is a small and ordinary. . . it is one thing and one thing only: it is doing what you have to do.

CHERYL STRAYED, NOVELIST

I'm here to tell you that if you get broken, it is possible to put yourself back together. I'm here to tell you that if you get lost, it is possible that a light will. . . lead you home.

NICK LAKE, NOVELIST

Achieving recovery is the ultimate goal when treating any disease, and schizophrenia is no exception. The following considerations may be helpful to understand how recovery may be possible and what it might look like for patients with schizophrenia.

Recovery is fluidly defined. Patients with schizophrenia should be able to play an active role in directing their care and live as independently as possible. These notions are relatively recent, and are indicative of a major shift away from the old way of thinking that it was not possible to achieve full recovery and reintegration into society.

Recovery may require accommodations. Think about a person diagnosed with polio; the sufferer may require a wheelchair for the rest of his or her life, but with some adjustments, he or she can live a full life. Similarly, a person with schizophrenia may need adaptations (that are available) to make it possible to be considered recovered and to participate in life in a meaningful way.

Recovery is not a straight line. While some patients with schizophrenia respond to treatment in a way that can be considered as fully recovered following their first episode, it is much more common to have occasional bumps in the road that require reevaluation and adjustment of treatment.

In addition to medical and psychosocial treatments, there are patient-related, treatment-related, biological, and environmental factors that researchers have identified as affecting recovery.

FACTORS INFLUENCING RECOVERY POTENTIAL

Recovery from schizophrenia, no matter how you define it, cannot be guaranteed. And while the following factors may influence whether recovery at any level is possible, it is important to note that they neither assure success nor doom a patient to failure. Patients with positive family ties, for example, are more likely to experience symptom remission, though that does not mean that those with no close family relationships will not achieve recovery. Each of these factors plays a role in recovery, but on their own, they do not tell the full story regarding a patient's potential outcomes.

Access to care. Unsurprisingly, a patient's ability to access continuous, consistent treatment makes for more successful outcomes. Patients also benefit from the ability to access different modes of care (including prescription medications, individual and group therapy, and rehabilitation programs).

Cognitive abilities. Patients who maintain adequate cognitive skills (e.g., working memory, perception skills, and problem-solving abilities) tend to have stronger recovery outcomes than those without these functional abilities.

Duration of untreated psychosis. Patients who experience delays in the treatment of their initial psychotic episode may experience a greater difficulty in achieving remission or recovery, compared to those who enter treatment quickly.

Family relationships. Strong, supportive family ties provide emotional support that has been known to decrease the risk of potential relapse. Patients who lack these support systems or experience significant family stress have an increased risk of relapse.

Initial response to medication. The way a patient responds to the first round of treatments tried plays a role in predicting potential outcomes; patients who have good responses to the first antipsychotic drug (APD) report the most successful outcomes.

Personal history. A number of characteristics of an individual's history contribute to better recovery: later age at onset of illness, higher levels of functioning before diagnosis, a higher IQ, a college degree, and a strong work history.

Substance abuse. Nearly half of all patients with schizophrenia abuse alcohol, street drugs, or prescription medications, despite the fact that substance abuse issues are associated with higher rates of relapse and lower rates of recovery.

Social skills. Moderate to severe deficits in social skills are associated with unfavorable outcomes, though it is unclear whether this effect is due to the patient's willingness to work with care teams and comply with treatment plans or other mechanisms.

Supportive therapy. Almost all patients with schizophrenia who experience recovery report regularly attending individual and group therapy, in addition to having positive relationships with their clinical team members.

Treatment adherence. As mentioned throughout this book, nonadherence to established treatment plans does not bode well for short-term remission or long-term recovery.

CONDITIONS COMPLICATING RECOVERY

Recovery from schizophrenia can be hampered by several complicating factors (referred to by clinicians as "co-morbid" conditions).

Depression
Depression occurs in roughly 25–40% of patients with schizophrenia and is associated with increased suicidal tendencies and other poor outcomes. Depressive symptoms may precede schizophrenic experiences, may occur at the same time, or may follow the first psychotic episode (referred to as "postpsychotic depression").

As of yet, the relationship between these two diseases is not fully known. Depression in patients with schizophrenia may occur as sufferers come to grips with the nature of the illness and its lifetime implications. It may also be an integral part of schizophrenia itself, or reflect another disorder (e.g., schizoaffective disorder or major depression) occurring alongside schizophrenia. Patients experiencing their first schizophrenic episode tend to have more severe depression than those who go through multiple episodes; unsurprisingly, persistent hopelessness following hospital discharge is associated with poorer outcomes a year after diagnosis.

Seeing depressive symptoms in patients with schizophrenia presents clinicians with a diagnostic challenge. Depression accompanying psychosis is commonly seen in patients experiencing major depression, as well as in those going through the depressive phase of bipolar disorder. Other conditions, including neuroleptic-induced Parkinsonism and primary negative symptoms, can also be mistaken for depression.

Regardless of these challenges, co-morbid depression must be identified and treated promptly in order to improve overall outcomes. Typically, this is done through the use of selective serotonin reuptake inhibitors (SSRIs), which tend to be better tolerated than older antidepressants. Should antidepressant-resistant depression occur, atypical APDs like clozapine have proven more helpful than typical APDs.

Substance Abuse

Substance abuse is very common in patients with schizophrenia, with as many as 50% of patients abusing drugs or alcohol at some point. This rate is much higher than the general population. The most commonly abused illicit drug is marijuana. Alcohol and cocaine are commonly abused as well. The risk for substance abuse tends to be higher with young males, particularly those with less education. Substance abuse can occur at any time—before the onset of psychosis, during, or after the initial episode. Regardless of when substance abuse occurs, it has many negative consequences:

- Less effective medical treatment
- Treatment nonadherence and higher rates of relapse
- Increased risk of violence and suicide
- Risk of medical problems and injury
- Increased environmental problems (financial, housing, legal)

Abstaining fully from substances is not easy for abusers and often requires an integrated approach to both assessment and treatment. Expect that your care team will screen for substance abuse by asking the patient directly about substance usage or by gathering information through urine screening and other sources. If discovered, proper treatment for substance abuse in patients with schizophrenia may include further education, mechanisms that enhance the sufferer's motivation to quit, psychological intervention with cognitive behavior therapy or other approaches, or the prescription of atypical APDs like clozapine to minimize the desire to abuse substances.

Smoking

Interestingly, rates of cigarette smoking in patients with schizophrenia are roughly two to three times higher than the U.S. population at large. In fact, it is estimated that the prevalence of cigarette smoking in patients with schizophrenia is between 70 and 90%, compared with 35–55% for other patients with psychiatric disorders, and about 20% for the general population.

Although it is not entirely clear why these disparities in cigarette smoking rates exist, some of the reasons suggested include a genetic basis that makes cigarettes more desirable, the use of cigarettes as a means of self-medication, or an underlying neurobiological cause. Lending credence to these theories are observations that many patients start smoking after their first schizophrenic episode and that the nature of their smoking habits tend to differ from other smokers. Patients with schizophrenia, for example, tend to smoke higher-tar cigarettes and inhale more deeply compared to other cigarette users.

Supporting the idea of cigarettes as a means of self-medication is the observed effect that smoking activates liver enzymes that lower the blood levels of many psychoactive medications, reducing the side effects (including involuntary muscle contractions, feelings of restlessness, and muscle tremors) that often occur with their usage. As a result, the dosing of these medications must be adjusted to a patient's smoking level. Quitting suddenly could result in a dramatic increase in toxicity, while adopting a smoking level could render a previously successful dose ineffective.

PREVENTING RELAPSES

Aside from aiming for overall recovery, the goal of ongoing schizophrenia treatment includes minimizing short-term relapses as well. Effective treatment of the conditions described earlier may prevent future episodes from occurring entirely, but as schizophrenia is a disease with ups and downs that may occur with no identifiable cause, it is in everybody's best interest to understand what factors can prompt a relapse, as well as how oncoming relapses can be identified and headed off.

As a rule, the most common cause of schizophrenic relapses is under-medication, either because the patient has stopped following the prescribed treatment plan or because changes in the patient's illness require more medication than is being given. Increasing the assigned dosage at the first sign of a potential relapse may prevent a full-blown episode, which makes it important for patients to learn how to identify the signs and symptoms that indicate a relapse is imminent.

Apart from stopping medicines, other important reasons for relapse include substance abuse, stress, and sleep loss—all these factors begin with the letter "S," so just remember the four Ss to avoid!

Nevertheless, identifying the signs of relapse risk is complicated by the fact that every patient undergoes a different pre-relapse path. Some patients may experience changes in their sleep cycles, while others become more irritable, more confused, or more uncomfortable in new situations. A very comprehensive assessment gauge, called *Early Signs Scale* developed by Dr. Max Birchwood and colleagues in 1989, has been used extensively all over the world (see Appendix D for complete scale). A shorter version, developed by Dr. Jorgenson in 1998, and called *Warning Signals Scale*, has some value for us because it is very short (Table 11.1).

Answering yes to any of the questions on this survey could indicate an approaching relapse. The greater the number of symptoms being experienced, the stronger is the likelihood.

Table 11.1 Warning Signals Scale (WSS)

Have You Been Having Any of the Following?	No	Yes
My sleep has been restless or unsettled		
I have been feeling tense, afraid, or unsettled		
I have been having difficulty concentrating		
I have been feeling irritable or quick-tempered		
I have been feeling unable to cope with everyday tasks or interests		
I have been feeling tired or lacking energy		
I have been feeling depressed or low		
I have been feeling confused or puzzled		

Source: Jorgensen P (1998): Schizophrenic delusions: the detection of warning signals. *Schizophr Res* 22; 32(1): 17–22.

However, since no scale or survey can ever capture your specific situation, it is important to take responsibility for identifying your own unique patterns of symptoms that indicate an impending relapse, and create your own personalized *list of risk indicators*. Your care team can help you create such a list. Review it regularly, and share this with your caregivers.

MAINTAINING THE RIGHT ATTITUDE

The fact that recovery cannot be guaranteed and that relapses cannot always be prevented can lead to feelings of hopelessness among patients and their families. And when coupled with the understanding that schizophrenia is a lifelong illness, it is easy to see how sufferers and their support networks can feel devastated by this diagnosis.

And while it would be unethical of us to offer false hope regarding schizophrenia outcomes, we can say with complete certainty that many patients go on to live rich and rewarding lives after their diagnoses. In many cases, these positive outcomes occur when sufferers and their families adjust their expectations as they begin to accept the role the disease could play in their lives. It may be unrealistic to expect complete recovery in all cases, but in every situation, it is still possible to take pleasure in small changes and moderate improvements, like riding the bus alone for the first time or returning to work through supported employment programs. Some sufferers even go on to embrace the extra experiences they have and the unique outlook they develop on the world, precisely as the result of their schizophrenia.

In the next section of this book, we will look at more of the challenges associated with living with schizophrenia, as well as at the coping strategies that can help patients, their clinicians, and their support networks to overcome these struggles. In the meantime, try to maintain a positive attitude. No family wants to be forced to confront a chronic illness—either physical or mental. Through education, planning, adherence to treatment, and ongoing effort, it is possible to navigate the condition in a sustainable, satisfying way that respects the needs of both patients and their caregivers.

SUMMARY

- Recovery assessment and treatment planning must occur on an *individual* basis, since each patient has factors specific to him or her.
- Conditions occurring alongside schizophrenia, such as depression and substance abuse, can negatively impact outcome. Therefore it's important to address these issues in a timely manner.

- Several factors—some specific to the patient and others related to the environment—have been identified as influencing recovery. For example, good access to healthcare, getting early treatment, staying in treatment, and avoiding substance abuse positively impact recovery.
- Patients with schizophrenia have higher than usual rates of cigarette smoking, which may interfere with blood levels of prescription treatments. Quitting smoking helps patients to maintain consistent dosage requirements, while also minimizing the additional health risks associated with the practice.
- Relapse is a concern for all patients with schizophrenia, even after co-morbid conditions are accounted for and treated. Tracking symptom patterns and maintaining appropriate medication doses, though they cannot be avoided in all cases, can minimize potential relapses.
- Although recovery and relapse prevention cannot be guaranteed, they can be managed. It can be difficult to maintain a positive attitude in the face of this chronic illness, but schizophrenia is not a death sentence. With proper care, many patients go on to experience some level of recovery that can and should be celebrated.

SECTION 4

Coexisting with Schizophrenia

Life with Schizophrenia
Assembling Your Care Team
A Manual for Caregivers
Common Problems in Facing Schizophrenia
Managing Crises

CHAPTER 12

Life with Schizophrenia

Being challenged in life is inevitable, being defeated is optional.
ROGER CRAWFORD, ONLY ATHLETE WITH FOUR IMPAIRED LIMBS
TO COMPETE IN AN NCAA DIVISION AND CERTIFIED BY THE
U.S. PROFESSIONAL TENNIS ASSOCIATION

This section examines the many emotional and lifestyle issues that arise as a consequence of having schizophrenia, and having to confront the day-to-day realities of this disorder beyond the issue of medical treatment. Every person with schizophrenia, or the family member, will have a unique set of issues that can only be addressed in a manner that's specific to him or her. Yet, there are themes that appear regularly among patients and families, which we address here.

FACING YOUR DIAGNOSIS

The initial reaction to being given a diagnosis of schizophrenia can, understandably, be shock, denial, anger, sorrow, or all of these emotions! On the other hand, there may be a sense of relief in knowing that there is an "explanation" for what you or a relative may be going through. You will find yourself wondering what this diagnosis means for your ability to hold down a job in the future, or how watching your relative's potential decline might affect you emotionally. You may be struggling to reconcile all the different ways your diagnosis will affect your relationships with the people in your life.

But while it is unlikely that your initial reaction to this life-changing pronouncement will be positive, the way that you process this information and integrate it into your life will make a big difference in terms of your ability to cope with it. Keep the following suggestions in mind as you confront the reality of life after a schizophrenia diagnosis.

Getting to Know Your Illness Is Half the Battle Won!

If you are aware of your illness, and have accurate knowledge about this illness, you are already halfway to winning the battle! This actually represents a *starting point* without which proper treatment could not occur. As described in a previous section, getting an accurate diagnosis of schizophrenia isn't a quick or easy journey, and many patients with schizophrenia go undiagnosed indefinitely as a result. Be gratified that you have taken the first step toward potential recovery, even if the word "schizophrenia" was hard to hear.

Allow Room for Your Emotions

It is OK to be angry, sad, frustrated, or have other feelings you're experiencing following your diagnosis. It is not healthy to wallow in self-pity, but neither is it a good idea to repress your natural feelings. Consider journaling, meditating, or attending therapy sessions as helpful ways to process these emotions and make space for them, without allowing them to run your life.

Base Your Judgments on Current Data

Many of our instinctive responses to the word schizophrenia come from an outdated understanding of the disease, which conjures up images of patients locked in padded-wall mental hospitals. However, we've come a long way in our understanding of this disease. Patients today have access to many treatment options and care environments, and their odds of achieving recovery from symptoms are much higher as a result.

Avoid Blame Whenever Possible

Schizophrenia is a disorder of the brain; it is not something that a family member's behavior caused. If you are a parent, do not worry that your child-rearing approach was too lenient or too strict. And if you are the one with the illness, know that nothing your parents or anyone else did caused your disease. There is enough stress associated with a schizophrenia diagnosis. Do not add to it by assigning blame where none is due.

Try to Stay Positive

You may be a patient with schizophrenia, but *you are not your disease*! The success of the latest medications and therapies means that more patients go on to experience remission or reduction of symptoms than ever before. You can increase your odds of achieving this outcome by accessing the support resources available to you and sticking with your treatment plan.

Telling Others about the Diagnosis

While this may not be a priority early on, it is an issue that will certainly come up. Whether you want to let others know about the diagnosis, and with whom you share this, is entirely up to you. Keep in mind that we all are connected to people one way or another—families, friends, or communities. These people may raise questions; they may have noticed behavioral changes. If you do decide to share this information, you need to think about the consequences of sharing (positive and negative), when to do so, and importantly to what extent you share any details; your diagnosis is nobody's business but your own. If and when you're ready to talk to others about the diagnosis, it is important to choose the timing carefully and use appropriate level of communication (usually simple straightforward language). This process should never be rushed; enough time must be allowed to clarify points and emotionally process the news. The details about your condition should be shared on a need-to-know basis. For employers or schools, for example, "suffering from a medical condition" may suffice. On the other hand, you may want to open up more to close friends by saying that you have a "mental illness (or brain illness) that is treatable and poses no threat." One benefit of others (you trust) being aware of your diagnosis is that they can be support people in times of need.

RECOGNIZING SOURCES OF STRESS

No doubt that receiving a diagnosis of schizophrenia is challenging enough, and then there are a variety of stressors you may encounter along the way. It is important not to adopt a negative attitude or a sense of dread when it comes to dealing with these sources of stress. Focus instead on creating a plan for how you'll address them when—and if—they arise in your life.

Schizophrenia Is a Chronic Disease

Being diagnosed with any long-term disease can be a frightening, so do not be surprised if you find yourself asking "Why me?" or feeling sad at the prospect of having to manage your disease for the rest of your life. Schizophrenia can feel like an incredible burden, but it is important to remember that your care team, your medications, and your other therapies can all help carry the load. Remember always that *you are not alone* when it comes to coping with whatever comes along.

Schizophrenia Can Feel Disruptive to Family Life

When one is a newly diagnosed patient, learning that your disease has the potential to cause disruption in the lives of your family members may cause you stress. While at times it may be difficult to remember, do remind yourself that these people care for you, and want to help you to feel better.

Taking Daily Medication May Remind You of Your Condition

Medical therapies may have improved by leaps and bounds, yet these promising results do not necessarily make it any more agreeable to be stuck taking pills every day. Although the need for taking your medications regularly may remind you of your condition, and stress you, it is very important that you do not let this prevent you from sticking to your medication schedule and keeping up with your appointments. Even if you're feeling better as the result of your treatments, it is still important to keep up with your doctor's recommendations to avoid a relapse.

Schizophrenia Symptoms, Like Life, Can Be Somewhat Unpredictable

Certainly, we would all benefit from knowing the exact course of the disease, and how long symptoms last when they do come on. But since none of us can ever predict what the next day will be like, it is important to keep things in perspective. Not knowing whether tomorrow is going to be a good day or a bad one can be frustrating, but it is human. Be gentle with yourself and try to remember that your "down" days won't last forever.

Making Friends or Having a Girlfriend or Boyfriend May Seem Difficult

Making friends might be difficult sometimes because of the mistrustfulness and lack of motivation caused by the symptoms of schizophrenia. However, medication treatments and psychotherapy, such as social skills training, and CBT can help overcome the roadblocks to making and maintaining satisfying relationships.

Maintaining a Care Team Can Be Difficult

A good care team includes a number of different professionals, from therapists to psychiatrists to caseworkers and more. In addition, consistency is important, with patients benefiting most from a team that is both committed to top-quality care and stable in nature. But unfortunately, everything from insurance changes to medical staffing problems can disrupt the care environment. Losing a great provider (or your entire care team) is a very real concern for patients, and it is one that should be addressed sensitively by all those supporting the patient, should it occur.

Certainly, with a disease as complex as schizophrenia, this isn't an exclusive list of potential sources of stress. However, the steps needed to minimize the impact of these stressors tend to be the same, whether you're facing one of the specific situations described earlier or any of the other curveballs this disease can throw at you. Planning *ahead of time* for managing difficult situations will make you more confident in your ability to handle them as they occur. Educating your support network on your disease can help as well. And seeking care and support for your emotional well-being—in addition to the medical aspects of your condition—can give you the tools needed to manage your physical and mental health as you weather the storms this disease may bring.

SUMMARY

- The proper management of schizophrenia involves treating the complete person, not just medications and other therapies, but also his or her emotional responses, stressors, and lifestyle challenges.
- The initial reaction to the schizophrenia diagnosis may range from anger to sadness or from disbelief to relief. All reactions are appropriate, though it is important not to get bogged down in self-pity.
- It is up to you and your care team to decide when and how you disclose your illness to others. Family members and friends should not push you to do so if you do not feel comfortable doing so.
- Schizophrenia involves a number of different sources of stress beyond the initial diagnosis. Planning ahead for these challenges and educating your support network can help you cope.
- Try to maintain a positive outlook when facing your illness. Schizophrenia treatments have come a long way in the last 50 years, making everything from small improvements to complete remission of symptoms possible for patients.

CHAPTER 13

Assembling Your Care Team

Coming together is a beginning. Keeping together is progress.
Working together is success.
HENRY FORD, FOUNDER OF THE FORD MOTOR COMPANY

In the event of a crisis, assembling a *care team* may be the furthest thing from your mind—and rightfully so. In an emergency situation, the most important issue is getting you or your relative the treatment needed to keep all parties involved safe and healthy. However, once the crisis has passed, or if you've just received a diagnosis of schizophrenia, it is important to take the time now to build a care team—professionals whose judgments you trust. It makes managing the disease much easier, particularly if there are unexpected crises. Read through this chapter to learn who typically belongs on a care team.

If you have a health plan, it is important to find out what mental health services are covered, usually by contacting the plan's customer service team. Seeking psychiatric care without going through the necessary channels established by your plan may result in appointments and treatments not being covered by your insurance.

WHO BELONGS ON YOUR TEAM?

Schizophrenia is a complex condition that is no longer treated with medications alone. However, since medications are usually the first treatment approach, a psychiatrist will likely be your primary point of contact. Beyond that, your care team will also include professionals who help with everything from securing housing to returning to work. Depending on the specific needs of the patient, the care team may include the following.

Psychiatrists

Psychiatrists are physicians who have completed an additional training in psychiatric medicine after completing medical school. This training enables them to evaluate, diagnose, and prescribe the appropriate medications. Psychiatrists may be either Doctors of Medicine (MDs) or Doctors of Osteopathy (DOs), and they may specialize in particular fields of care, such as adolescent psychiatry or geriatric psychiatry.

Primary Care Physicians

Although your psychiatrist will probably be the one leading your relative's care, you may be in a situation (a remote location) that you have access only to your primary care physician, or PCP. These physicians typically are specialized in family or internal medicine. They may be able to provide perfectly adequate care, yet there may be situations where a mental health professional is required. Your PCP can help coordinate such referrals.

Social Workers

Another key member of your care team is a clinical social worker. Social workers may work privately, or be employed by your insurance company, hospital, or rehabilitation program. In any case, their role on your care team is to help you or your relative navigate the medical system, and access important benefits.

Case Managers

Case managers work in a similar capacity as social workers, though, unlike these related professionals, they may provide services directly to patients. They may also work in teams to help link patients to services such as rehabilitation programs, housing opportunities, and job training sessions. Most case managers work through programs funded by the state or federal government and use a framework called Assertive Community Treatment (ACT) to facilitate care.

Unfortunately, the demand for case management services often exceeds the supply of available case managers. To find case management programs in your area, contact your local public mental health authority. If you find that ACT or other programs exist near you but do not have immediate availability, be proactive about adding your relative to the program's waitlist and following up frequently to secure enrollment as quickly as possible. Be patient, but diligent. Working in conjunction with citizen advocacy groups in your area can help you secure these important services as well.

Other Professionals

Depending on your insurance coverage, your local medical system, and your relative's unique situation, you may find that any of the following types of professionals play a role on your care team. In most cases, you will be assigned to or referred to these providers by one of the providers listed earlier.

Psychologists and counselors. Psychotherapy alone is not considered an appropriate treatment plan for schizophrenia, although some counseling programs can be used successfully alongside treatment with antipsychotics and other medications. If your psychiatrist or PCP recommends seeking out these services, ask whether or not they have experience treating patients with schizophrenia. Some states have very lax requirements regarding the education and training required using the title *therapist* or *psychotherapist*, and working with an inexperienced professional may do more harm than good.

Psychiatric nurses. Whether you receive treatment in a private practice, clinic, or hospital setting, you will likely work closely with one or more psychiatric nurses. These professionals are generally well experienced with schizophrenia, its treatments, and the side effects that are common to antipsychotic use, making them an important part of your care team. In most cases you will work with a psychiatric nurse assigned to your psychiatrist or primary care doctor.

Treatment-specific therapists. Throughout the course of treatment, your care team or case manager may refer you to treatment-specific therapists who will aid particular aspects of your care. A few of these professionals that you may encounter include occupational therapists (who help patients learn or relearn skills needed for daily living), vocational therapists (who assist patients in returning to the workforce), rehabilitation therapists (who may support patients with everything from developing social skills to ensuring proper money management), and recreation therapists (who engage patients in activities like photography, woodworking, sports, or crafts to meet their emotional and cognitive needs).

Peer counselors. Many cities and towns have peer-counseling programs, through which fellow mental illness sufferers, who have been trained to facilitate group or one-on-one therapy, share their experiences and serve as role models for recovery. Any member of your care team or your local public mental health authority should be familiar with any such programs in your area and should be able to provide referrals when appropriate.

While these auxiliary treatment providers will likely be assigned to or referred to you, you may need to select the higher-level clinicians who will do the referring on their own. Building your team, therefore, begins with the search for the psychiatrist or primary care physician who will oversee your care.

BUILDING YOUR TEAM

Knowing the types of professionals you'll work with throughout your course of treatment is only the first step of the journey. Next, you'll need to review the different professionals who are active in your area and select the providers you trust and with whom you feel most comfortable.

Check with Your Insurance Provider

If you have an insurance plan that will be responsible for covering all or part of your care, whether a private plan or insurance through a public program like Medicaid, your first step should be to contact your plan's customer support team to ask for a list of providers that accept your insurance. It is also important to ask whether your plan requires a referral to see a psychiatrist or if you can access these services directly. Working with approved providers will minimize—if not eliminate entirely—the amount of money you'll be responsible for paying out of pocket.

Assemble a Short List

If insurance will be covering you or your relative's treatment, the list of approved providers you receive represents your short list of potential care providers. But if you are not limited to a specific number of professionals you'll need to build this list yourself. There are several resources you can consult to put together your own short list of providers. Begin by asking any friends, family members, or acquaintances you know who have dealt with mental health issues for recommendations. Soliciting personal referrals is a great way to identify potential care team members who are both knowledgeable about schizophrenia and whose personalities and treatment approaches will match your expectations.

If you are not able to gather any personal referrals, contact your local National Alliance on Mental Health (NAMI) chapter or use websites like www.HealthGrades.com or www.Vitals.com for reviews on local mental health professionals. As you review these options, consider carefully whether you or your relative require special services (as an example, elderly patients may benefit from seeing geriatric psychiatrists), or whether the patient has a preference for their providers to be of a specific age or gender. In either of these cases, seeking out clinicians who meets the patient's expectations increases the odds of developing a trusting relationship that supports ongoing treatment adherence.

Questions to Ask about Treatment Providers

If the possibility exists, you should conduct in-person interviews to get a feel for the provider (can you work with this person?). However, this will be rare because providers may not have the time or there may be no way to bill for just an interview without providing a clinical service. Thus, you may get answers to key questions only by calling the office, checking their website, or asking around. You may have many questions for the provider, but the following is a good start:

What are your credentials? Are they psychiatrists? Are they board certified (it means they have passed a national exam in this specialty)?

How much experience do you have treating patients with schizophrenia? When a choice exists, a psychiatrist with experience in treating patients with schizophrenia may be better for you.

What types of insurance do you accept? If your insurance company has referred you to a particular provider, obviously the provider accepts your insurance. However, if you are choosing clinicians who do not accept your insurance plan (or take insurance payments altogether), ask about "sliding scale" payments or payment plans based on your income.

What is your general treatment approach for schizophrenia? Though the prescription of antipsychotic medications is fairly standard, many clinicians will include a variety of therapies as part of the overall treatment plan. Some clinicians offer both services within a single setting (which may be more convenient for patients who are reluctant to visit multiple providers), while others will coordinate your care with additional providers.

How do you handle emergencies? This is important information! While it may be unpleasant to think about future crises, knowing how your provider manages emergencies can help you to feel more confident in planning for and handling crises. At a minimum, your clinician should have some sort of system in place to guide you through a crisis. It is common for providers to have 24-hour emergency telephone numbers that will provide instructions. These could be access to a backup provider, instructions to contact the nearest psychiatric or general emergency service, or even same-day appointments. Regardless, you should have this information with you at all times (keep a card in your wallet as well as somewhere easily accessible). Calling 9-1-1, or similar emergency services in other countries, should be the last resort.

Once you've identified the psychiatrist or primary care doctor that will lead your care team, notify your insurance plan of your selection (if required) and contact the provider's office to schedule your first appointment. Keep in mind that some providers may be booked out for several weeks or months. If it is important for you to be seen sooner, speak with the provider's office about alternative arrangements or select another clinician.

WHEN YOUR TEAM ISN'T WORKING

In an ideal world, the care team you have will be the right fit from the start, and will continue to function smoothly for the duration of your treatment. However, certain situations may arise that could disrupt your care, such as:

- Disagreements with members of care team regarding the appropriate course of treatment
- Feeling that your care team is not listening to or acknowledging your concerns
- Decisions influencing the course of treatment that are made without your knowledge or approval
- Poor communication between team members that results in important information about your symptoms, side effects, or complications not being transferred

Then there are situations beyond anyone's control, but have a direct impact on your care, such as:

- Care team members relocating or leaving the practice
- Changes in insurance that are not accepted by your providers

In such instances, your care team or insurance company should help you make a smooth transition to a new care team or providers.

If you find yourself facing the issues just mentioned, or any others, take the following steps:

Make your concerns known. Too often patients and families simply walk away from a care team that they are having difficulty with, but the consequences of this are very serious. Instead, talk to your providers about any concerns you have. In many instances, frustrations with care team members stem from simple miscommunications or misunderstandings. If, for example, you feel you're being left out of important conversations, it could be that your clinicians did not realize you wanted to be included or did not know the best way to relay information to you. Clearing the air, when possible, can prevent you from having to go through the more time-consuming process of selecting new care team members.

Make care team changes, only if absolutely necessary. If voicing your concerns reveals fundamental problems that can't be resolved or compromise care (e.g., if your provider's treatment protocols are out-of-date or if he or she has no system to manage crises), you may need to go through the process of selecting care team members again. Transferring your care to a new clinician should never be done casually; such transitions are time-consuming, require new therapeutic alliances, and acquainting yourself with the way your new team functions.

Remember, the vast majority of mental health clinicians place the highest premium on excellent patient care. But like so many healthcare workers, psychiatrists and other clinicians work in environments with limited resources and within overburdened medical systems. For you this means that some amount of patience is required. However, your care should never be compromised. Raise your concerns as needed, but also make it a point to positively recognize those professionals who go above and beyond on your behalf.

SUMMARY

- In an emergency situation, your clinicians will probably be assigned by the emergency room or psychiatric hospital where you're being seen. After discharge, you may be recommended to follow up with your regular doctor, if you have one. Otherwise, you may be given referrals. In any event, you will want to select your care team and clinicians in a thoughtful manner.
- A psychiatrist or primary care doctor will lead your care team. Other members of your care team may include psychologists, social workers, case managers, psychiatric nurses, treatment-specific therapists, peer counselors, and more.
- Begin the process of building your care team by consulting with your insurance provider (if applicable), since the plan may limit whom you are permitted to see.
- If there are insurance restrictions, ask for referrals from friends, family members, or acquaintances. You can also contact your local NAMI chapter or consult medical professional review websites for suggestions.
- Determine how well the clinicians fit with your treatment and personal expectations.
- A number of issues can disrupt the proper functioning of a care team, such as clinicians leaving the practice or failure to communicate treatment plans appropriately. Raising your concerns may be enough to resolve these issues, though in some cases, seeking out new clinicians may be necessary.

CHAPTER 14

A Manual for Caregivers

Never give up on someone with a mental illness. When "I" is replaced by "We," illness becomes wellness.

SHANNON L. ADLER, AUTHOR

Anyone—at any time—can find himself or herself thrust into the role of caregiver for someone with schizophrenia! Schizophrenia does not discriminate, nor does it always choose those sufferers whose family members or close friends are well suited to providing care. Most of us are unprepared for such a life-altering task. It requires a new mind-set, a new set of skills and knowledge, and reaching inwards for emotional resources. While each situation is unique, there are a few general themes that are common to being a caregiver.

Thus far, the preceding chapters of this book have provided information, principles, and guidelines that are relevant to both patients and caregivers. In this section we will focus primarily on the needs of caregivers. Few of you will enter your new role with medical backgrounds or experience in supportive capacities. For this reason, the aim of this section is to acquaint you with diverse ways in which caregivers support patients, the resources needed to be an effective caregiver, and the very real challenge of caregiver burnout.

THE ROLE OF THE CAREGIVER

The extent of your involvement as a caregiver will depend on the severity and chronicity of your relative's condition. A schizophrenia patient who experiences only a few isolated symptomatic episodes will, as you might expect, require a lesser level of attention than someone who has been rendered significantly disabled.

That said, many caregivers find themselves involved in the same core group of tasks, regardless of the patient's condition. These common needs may include the following:

Helping the patient attend doctor visits. Given the complexity of institutionalized medical systems and schizophrenia treatment plans, having a caregiver attend clinical meetings, as a patient advocate, can be extremely valuable. In this capacity, you may be called upon to transport the patient, ask the doctor questions, and be sure any recommended treatments are clearly outlined and understood.

Maintaining contact with the care team. On any given day, questions or pieces of information may need to be passed on to your patient's doctors. Status reports need to be given and medications need to be adjusted—and it will be up to you to relay this information promptly and correctly and to implement any suggestions made by your clinical team.

Creating healthy daily routines at home. Most patients benefit from having consistent routines, whether at home or alternative housing. As a caregiver, it will be your job to make sure these routines include healthy eating, personal care activities, and regular sleep cycles, as well as to ensure that the routines you (jointly) create are followed by your relative.

Making sure the patient is taking his or her medicine. It is very common to see, after improvements with treatment, the discontinuation of medication because the patients feel they no longer need it. This can make your job challenging, since preventing relapses may depend on your ability to get your relative to continue taking the recommended prescription at the appropriate dosage.

Early identification of worsening symptoms. Watching a patient's health decline can be disheartening and scary. However, as the caregiver, it will be up to you to detect these changes and report them back to your care team so that the appropriate interventions can be taken before the situation becomes dire.

One of the most difficult aspects of caregiving is that roughly half of all schizophrenia patients (and nearly the majority of them at some point in their illness) do not understand that they're unwell (a symptom known as *anosognosia*). Patients who do not believe they're ill often have diffi-culty following treatment plans, requiring caregivers to walk a fine line between respecting the patient's autonomy and enforcing necessary care. Watching a relative refuse the help he or she needs can be challenging, but it is important to remember that it is his or her disease—not him or her, personally—that causes him or her to act this way.

ARE YOU CAPABLE OF CAREGIVING?

Helping a patient meet his or her needs through the activities described earlier requires a variety of physical, emotional, and financial resources.

Time

How available can you be to the schizophrenia patient? Even if your relative maintains a high level of functioning, time spent attending doc-tor appointments and advocating for his or her care may require you to leave work or interrupt your other household responsibilities. Ask your-self the following questions before taking on the full- or part-time role:

- Does your employer offer sufficient vacation hours or personal leave time for you to attend medical appointments, maintain healthy rou-tines at home, or leave work suddenly in the event of a crisis? A fed-eral law—Family and Medical Leave Act (FMLA)—entitles employees to take unpaid, job-protected leave the family and medical reasons. Check with your employer whether you are eligible for this entitle-ment. If not, you may need to make other arrangements, such as mak-ing up work time.
- Will your company understand the need to prioritize a relative's health over work responsibilities, or will your advancement oppor-tunities suffer?
- If you stay at home caring for others, how will your added respon-sibilities to the patient impact your workload? Will you be able to cook, clean, and otherwise maintain your household while balanc-ing these new requirements? How will it affect other members in your household?

Do not feel that you must drop everything to become the only caregiver in your relative's life. This may not be feasible for a number of reasons, and other demands on your time deserve consideration in this decision. As discussed in Appendix C, a number of different resources are out there that can help supplement your caregiving efforts if you are unable or unwilling to manage this responsibility on your own.

Money

Caregiving expenses can add up quickly. Even the best health insurance in the world isn't unlimited, so it is possible you'll wind up paying copays, coinsurance, and other expenses out of pocket. If your relative lives with you, your costs for food, clothing, and other essentials could increase. Leaving your job to become a full-time caregiver negatively impacts your total income, while attending doctor visits increases your transportation costs and the wear on your vehicle as well.

It is easy to say, "I'll pay whatever it takes to care for my relative," but take some time to truly consider the financial ramifications of doing so. Although money matters are never easy to discuss, it is important to review your situation before any potential financial difficulties. There are legal experts who specialize in setting up trust funds for patients who are unable to manage funds on their own.

Knowledge

It is important to educate yourself about schizophrenia —its nature, its treatment, and about the issues specific to your relative's situation. However, it is vital to obtain this information from trustworthy sources, such as the care team, hospital websites, and other sources (many are listed in Appendix C). This information is valuable to put into context the behaviors you observe in your relative. Further, as an advocate for your relative may mean learning how to navigate complex medical, mental health, social service, and legal systems. You may enjoy reading scientific reports on developing treatments. If you feel overwhelmed by this prospect, remember that all this learning doesn't need to happen in one go—it is an ongoing process. At any time you do not understand something, you should feel completely free in asking the care team questions and clarifications. Inaccurate information or misinterpreting your observations can be troublesome.

Emotional Stability

You can have all the love in the world for your relative, but it is hard to deny that the reality of schizophrenia, at times, can be frustrating, and even disheartening. The person you knew before is now changed, hopefully in small ways, but sometimes in very significant ways. The person who used to be bubbly may now be withdrawn, with no apparent interest in connecting with others. It can be disturbing to see your relative battle with hallucinations. Facing these challenges, and heartaches, and sometimes even your own urge to withdraw from your relative, requires reaching into a deeper well of emotional resources. Looking out for his or her best interests takes emotional stability and resiliency. If you have concerns about your ability to provide this level of support, or if existing demands on you leave you without the emotional bandwidth needed to help a patient cope, consider seeking additional help from other family, friends, and even counselors.

Understand that there is no shame in acknowledging that you lack the necessary emotional resources to provide the level of care your relative may require, or the degree to which you want to be invested in such care. Although your initial impulse may be to give yourself over fully to caring for your relative, seeking the assistance of other caregivers or programs may make more sense in the long run. Nevertheless, since your top priority is his or her well-being, it is best to think through these issues, and perhaps even discuss them with the rest of the family.

AVOIDING CAREGIVER BURNOUT

Caregiver burnout—a state of physical, mental, and emotional exhaustion that is detrimental to both caregivers and patients—is a real issue. While everyone experiences some burnout at some point, the key is to

Figure 14.1 Caregiver Burden

minimize the risk of developing it, to reduce its severity, and to learn to cope effectively. Many caregivers cannot recognize when they are suffering burnout—it can sneak up on you. It can eventually get to the point where the caregiver cannot function effectively, and their health is jeopardized.

The primary reason for developing burnout is neglect of one's emotional and physical health while attending to the demands of caregiving. Additionally, there are other factors that contribute to a caregiver's burnout:

Unrealistic expectations. As a caregiver it is entirely normal to expect that the "service" you provide will have a positive effect on the course of illness and quality of life. In most cases this is probably true. However, this can lead to having unrealistic expectations about your capabilities, because the illness course can be unpredictable, and when things don't go quite right, you end up blaming yourself.

Unreasonable demands. Because of the urge to do your best, all of the time, it is a setup for burnout. Further, believing that you are the *only one* who can offer the best care adds to the burden. In some instances, there are others (family, friends, community) who may *expect* you to be the caregiver, regardless of your capacity to be one.

Confusion about your new role. Prior to the onset of the illness, your role probably was as a mother, or partner, or relative or friend. Now, however, you have an additional role: caregiver. Switching around your role from moment to moment can be confusing, and consequently stressful.

Lack of control. Having predictability in life, being able to choose and plan the future, allocating resources for different parts of one's life are the hallmarks of control over one's life. Even with the new role of a caregiver, one can feel "in control" when all aspects of care are going according to plan. However, when any of the several aspects of a controlled life (time, health, money, relationships) go awry—losing control—it can be highly stressful. Ongoing lack of control (unraveling) can be overwhelming, and lead to burnout.

How do you know you are suffering from burnout? If any of the following symptoms sound familiar, you could be experiencing caregiver burnout:

- Chronic exhaustion
- A change in attitude: from positive and caring to negative and indifferent

- Feelings of chronic anger toward your relative, and associated guilt
- Irritability
- Poor concentration and short-term memory, affecting normal chores and work
- Loss of interest in previously enjoyed activities
- Withdrawing from family and friends
- Changes in appetite or weight (could be more or less)
- Changes in sleep pattern, either sleeping too much or too little
- Experiencing more illnesses than usual, probably due to stress-related weakened immune system
- New or renewed substance abuse problems

If left unaddressed, caregiver burnout can be devastating for all involved. To prevent this insidious danger from affecting your ability to care for your relative, the following strategies may be helpful:

Make time for yourself. While you may feel guilty for taking time out for yourself at the possible expense of your relative, remember that *your well-being* is what allows you to be an effective caregiver in the first place. You may *feel* like there is no time available to you, but the truth is that there is always time, although you may need to plan in advance. Make an appointment with yourself! During this time do what you find revitalizing. For some it is a long walk alone, for others it may be going to the house of faith. Or it could be reading, a movie, a long warm shower, cooking, working on your hobby, gardening, etc. Only you can know what will help you regain a sense of balance in life; whatever it may, you need to practice it regularly, even when you do not necessarily feel overwhelmed.

Respite. Sometimes just taking occasional timeouts for you yourself may not be enough. In such situations, respite may be what you need. Having a spouse or relative or a friend take over caregiving duties for a day, or several days, can offer you a much-needed break.

Be realistic. Schizophrenia is a complex illness, and its course and treatment response can be unpredictable, so it is essential to be realistic—about *your* capacity to guide its course. And be accepting of the fact that your relative may also have little control over what they experience. At some level, neither of you can stop delusions or hallucinations from occurring, nor can you talk him or her out of symptoms like flat affect or lack of motivation. There's no point in banging your head against matters that are unalterable or uncontrollable; it is much more fruitful to direct your energies toward things you can change.

Make sure your role is clear. Confusion among multiple caregivers is a recipe for stress and tension. If you share caregiving roles with others—including those that are part of your medical care team—have a clear understanding about where one person's responsibilities end and another's begin. Such confusion is not only stressful but can also be detrimental to patient care.

Do not take it personally. If you're caring for a patient with whom you have a personal relationship, it can be difficult to separate your role as caregiver from your position as spouse, parent, child, or friend. Do your best to keep these identities separate, and do not be afraid to call in reinforcements if you need time away from the situation to redraw your boundaries.

Practice self-compassion. In other words, forgive yourself. Neither you nor anyone else caused schizophrenia. It is normal to have "bad" feelings about the situation you find yourself in. Beating yourself over feelings or these situations only increase anger and depression. It is better to acknowledge these negative feelings, and move on. This means a *nonjudgmental acceptance* of these thoughts, your limitations and weaknesses, your mistakes, regrets, and unspoken desires. It is simply human to experience these feelings. Hanging on to these notions can grind you down, and add to misery. It is better to have true *self-acceptance* that will enable you to overcome constant negativity.

CONTINUITY OF CARE

If you are the primary caregiver, it is important that you consider how continuity of care would be provided if you were somehow incapacitated. There *will* be situations that will prevent you—temporarily or indefinitely—from continuing to be a primary caregiver: illness, new job requirements, financial constraints, or family members in a worse situation. It could be anything, and when it happens, it is almost always unplanned!

For most caregivers, however, one issue more than any other is the hardest to voice—one's own mortality. It is quite natural to struggle with this issue. None of us necessarily go about our lives thinking about death and dying. However, not addressing this eventuality will have consequences for continuity of care of your son or daughter. Regardless of good intentions, caregivers can leave gaps in *future care plans*, by making assumptions that caregiving will be assumed by someone else in the family, such as a sibling. It is better for everyone involved to get advice from a variety of resources such as legal and advisory help that are readily available.

At a minimum, the following questions should get you thinking about continuity of care:

- If you are unable to continue providing care, who will take over your responsibilities?
- Are the people you have identified suited to caregiving roles?
- Have they agreed to their future role?
- How might these people be compensated?
- How will expenses for caregiving be handled?
- If your relative lives with you, where will he or she live if you are unable to remain in your home?
- Who will make medical decisions for your relative?
- Do you have up-to-date information about your charge (in a folder or computer file) to facilitate seamless transition to the next caregiver?

Depending on your answers to these questions, you may find it helpful to seek the assistance of a qualified attorney who can help you draft powers of attorney documentation, guardianship agreements, health-care proxies, and any other legally binding agreements needed to protect your relative's interests, should you become incapacitated. A financial advisor may also be of assistance in setting up *supplemental needs trusts* and other investment vehicles that will fund your relative's future care.

Planning for the inevitable may be unpleasant, but it should be treated as one of the key responsibilities of a primary caregiver. Beyond that, everyone—family and friends, the care team, the community—will be beyond grateful for your service!

SUMMARY

- Anyone, at any time, can be thrust into a caregiving position.
- Potential caregivers must determine whether they have the time, money, knowledge, and emotional stability to be effective in this role.
- There is no shame in admitting that you may not be up to the task of full- or part-time caregiving. However, if you are in this position, you must try to put the patient's needs first. This may mean accepting help and seeking out other resources.

- Caregiver burnout is a state of exhaustion that comes from putting more time and energy into patient care than is available to you, and not taking care of yourself in the process. Burnout can be hazardous to your mental and physical health.
- Preventing caregiver burnout is vital to the long-term stability of the patient-caregiver relationship and involves taking personal time, adjusting expectations, and clarity of responsibilities.
- Caregivers must develop a plan of action for continuity of care in the event they become incapacitated. This action plan should make use of legal and financial tools to help provide for the patient in their absence.

CHAPTER 15

Common Problems in Facing Schizophrenia

> We don't get to choose the things that happen to us in life. What we can choose is how to react to them, how we deal with them, and how we move on.
>
> SARAH WINTER, *SNOWBOUND*

You do not need a book to tell you that facing schizophrenia or assisting a relative who is going through the process can be challenging. Like any other mental disorder, schizophrenia has the potential to disrupt many aspects of life—relationships, school, work, leisure, and personal growth.

In this chapter we will focus on solutions to common problems encountered during the course of illness. Shortly on after the onset of symptoms, the focus tends to be on initiating treatment and get under control of the most disruptive symptoms, managing side effects if there are any, and starting the stabilization process. Depending upon the rapidity of treatment response, issues related to longer-term challenges could be addressed during convalescence. The set of problems that emerge are unique to each patient. There are many factors that will determine this, such as premorbid functioning, degree of family support, and treatment adherence.

There are a number of issues that tend to occur relatively frequently; these can be broadly categorized as *symptom-specific, behavioral*, and *structural*. Symptom-specific issues relate primarily to persistent delusions and hallucinations. Behavioral issues can be highly varied, but common challenges include managing stress, interpersonal communication, socialization, and substance abuse. Structural issues often reflect the immediate environment of the patient (e.g., living situation), as well as finances, negotiating the healthcare systems, schooling and work.

The key to success in dealing with these problems is early recognition, and anticipating potential issues before they become emergencies. It is important to remind yourself that you are *not* alone in facing these issues.

MANAGING CHRONIC SYMPTOMS

About a third of patients experience persistent hallucinations and delusions, despite optimal treatment, which may be quite distressing. Some strategies may be helpful, which are listed in Tables 15.1 and 15.2.

Table 15.1 ABCs of Coping with Hallucinations

Arousal reduction	Relaxation and deep breathing exercises Blocking ears, closing eyes Listening to music
Behavior	Increasing other activities Mentally separating the *real you* from the voices Asking trusted people about the reality of the voices
Cognition	Distracting, normal activities Ignoring the voices Positive self-talk (the voices are *not* you!)

Source: Modified from Reddy and Keshavan, 2006.

Table 15.2 Delusions BARRED

Become aware	Don't try to shy away from becoming aware of delusional (false) thoughts and assumptions. Being aware will help you counter these false beliefs.
Alternative explanations	Use substitute (more neutral) explanations for delusional thoughts. If you hear a group of people laughing, don't assume they are laughing at you—they are simply laughing at each other!
Record	Keep track of delusional thoughts and write them down.
Relaxation techniques	Learn to use deep breathing as well as distraction techniques (e.g., listening to music, exercising, chatting with friends).
Esteem	You are *not* what the delusions or voices suggest you are! You are your own person, and you can improve self-esteem. Therapy is useful for this.
Double-book keeping	This is a mental trick of being able to keep your *real self* and ideas separated from false and unreal thoughts. If the false ideas don't go away with treatment, just acknowledge their presence but without giving in to them.

Source: Modified from Reddy and Keshavan, 2006.

BEHAVIORAL ISSUES

Reducing Stress

Stress is a normal part of the business of life. However, chronic stress is emotionally and physically bad. It appears that schizophrenia changes the capacity to tolerate stress, where seemingly common, everyday situations can feel highly stressful. Sometimes there's no awareness that there is ongoing stress. Regardless, it is also well known that excessive stress can worsen symptoms. Therefore, minimizing the risk of stressful situations is important, and may be accomplished by some of the following strategies:

Plan and stick to routines. Having consistent routines (habits) creates a safe environment; knowing in advance what the daily tasks are makes them automatic and easy to plan the day, and therefore less stressful. While having daily routines is useful for everyone, it is particularly helpful for patients who have trouble remembering specific tasks, or have difficulty in figuring out what the next steps are in a given situation. We suggest putting together a morning routine, a regular daily activity schedule, and a series of bedtime habits to help minimize stress. Your care team or a caregiver can help with setting up routines.

Break down big tasks into small chunks. Whenever it is hard to maintain focus over longer periods of time, it is best to do anything in stages. Big projects should be broken down into smaller tasks, tackling each small piece one at a time, completing one small task before moving on to the next one. For example, do not try to clean the whole apartment all at one time. Break down the process into bits that can be done in 15 minutes at a time. Do not do the laundry the same time as washing dishes! Consider making lists of all the tasks you'd like to accomplish for the week; then break down this list to create a daily to-do list. We suggest breaking the daily list even further to some things that you can manage in the morning and some in the afternoon. The neat thing about this system is that you can look at the list and see for yourself that you'll be able to manage your goals. Check off tasks as you move forward with the activities—it a great feeling!

Exercise regularly. If you used to exercise regularly, get back to it. Regular physical activity is stress relieving and mood elevating. Even regular walk can have positive effects. Motivating yourself may be difficult, but if you build it into your daily routine, it might be easier to do.

Expect that bad days will occur. Expecting perfection from any person is a recipe for disaster, let alone a person suffering from schizophrenia. While you can take steps to reduce stress and help your relative develop appropriate coping skills, it is important to remember that bad days will occur. Be sensitive to the frustrations these bad days can present and reassure the patient that temporary challenges will pass.

Learn stress management techniques. Relaxation techniques, such as muscle relaxation and deep breathing exercises, can be learned easily, and are very helpful. Ask your therapist to teach you these simple techniques. Listening to calming music, or simply taking a walk, can also be very helpful.

PERSONAL AND SOCIAL COPING SKILLS

Schizophrenia tends to modify the capacity to relate to people. Even if the patient was quite social in the past, there is a tendency to reduce the social circle to a very small number of people, to a single person, or even to no one. This may be due to the 4 Ss:

Speech problems due to thinking disturbance
Social skills deteriorate due to the illness
Symptoms, such as paranoia or apathy
Stigma—rejection by others—that leads to further isolation

However, the shrinking social network can have many negative effects, including loneliness, depression, poor self-care, and onset of substance abuse. Therefore, it is vital that every effort—to the extent the patient can tolerate—should be made to decrease isolation by helping with communication and social skills:

Improving communication skills. Many schizophrenia symptoms make it challenging for patients to communicate effectively with others. Suspicious thoughts may cause them to be fearful of others. Medications may make them too drowsy to sustain a conversation. Even when interactions do occur, they may be disrupted by the inability to accurately process information, or carry out plans due to apathy. For this reason, helping a schizophrenia patient communicate better is as much about providing the time and space for conversations to occur as it is altering the way you engage her. For best results, choose an environment that is free of distractions and a time when both of you are in a healthy place mentally. If the patient is already stressed, or if you are feeling irritated, consider waiting until you are able to discuss important issues with clearer heads. Group therapy and other rehabilitative programs focus on this challenge, and should be part of the overall treatment plan.

Fostering independence. While caring for a patient can seemingly be all-encompassing endeavor, it is important not to let the pendulum swing so far that you end up doing for him or her what he or she is able to do for himself or herself. This has the potential to turn into *learned helplessness*, in which patients who are capable of participating in their own care and decision making become passive in the face of overeager caregivers. To help foster independence, engage patients in activities that help to build their self-esteem. This may be as simple as praising them for tasks they perform well on their own or as advanced as helping them to budget their own money (rather than providing an allowance or other entitlement). Encouraging patients to participate in self-help and peer support groups may also help them maintain their sense of self and independence.

DRUG AND ALCOHOL ABUSE

Drug and alcohol abuse are significant problems for the population at large, but they pose special challenges for schizophrenia patients, as substance abuse increases the likelihood that they will follow recommended treatment plans decreases, consequently leading to relapses. Patients may use drugs and alcohol to "self-medicate," to "escape" from the frustrating reality of chronic illness, or to create a social network with other users. Regardless of reasons for use, it can have many damaging effects.

Therefore, it is very important to have a straightforward and honest discussion with both patient and family together, about the dangers resulting from drug abuse and the possibility that the patient may abuse drugs. To avoid breaking confidentiality, it is best to get permission from the patient in advance to contact the care team, thus empowering the family members to stay in communication with the care team, before any problems come up.

If you suspect that your relative is using drugs or alcohol, take the following steps:

Alert care team. If drug or alcohol use is suspected, do not remain silent. If the care team is unaware, it is important that they know that the issue can be addressed early, and specific treatments can be instituted.

Make expectations clear. Educate the patient about the dangers of drug abuse, including the fact that symptom worsening may lead to hospitalization. Do not be needlessly harsh, but do set clearly defined limits of acceptable behavior.

Seek out additional treatment programs. Some schizophrenia patients may benefit from involvement in 6-step or 12-step programs, while inpatient rehabilitation stays may better serve others. The option that's right for your relative will depend on what's available in your community, your financial resources, and the patient's willingness to comply.

STRUCTURAL ISSUES
Money and Finances

It is natural to expect that, when confronting a relative's mental disorder, one of your first questions might be "How will he or she support himself or herself?" This question becomes especially important when medication, therapy sessions, supportive housing, and other needs are taken into consideration. The following are a number of ways in which help is available.

Supplemental Security Income (SSI) and Social Security Disability Insurance (SSDI)

SSI and SSDI are two programs issued by the Social Security Administration that provide a modest income to the needy elderly and disabled citizens. Both programs include schizophrenia patients in their definitions of disability, though, to be eligible for SSDI, the patient must have worked before his or her diagnosis. The amount of the benefits available depend on the number of hours worked before diagnosis in the case of SSDI and whether or not the patient's state of residence supplements federal dollars in the case of SSI.

Application for both programs can be made through your relative's local Social Security office, though you should be aware that it could take 3–6 months for a decision (and this comes after the months or years after receiving the initial diagnosis of schizophrenia). SSDI performs its own independent assessment of disability. The factors that go into decision making include evidence of significant impairment in capacity to perform routine and expected tasks, which prevent any form of employment

If your initial application is rejected, you do have the right to appeal, and it is recommended that you do so. Determining eligibility for SSI and SSDI payments is a subjective process, so getting another determination can increase chances of success. No matter how long your claim takes, payments will be made retroactively to the date of your application. Federal monthly SSI payments for 2015 are capped at $733 for an eligible individual and more for an eligible individual with an eligible spouse.

However, even if the patient's income level reduces his or her SSI and/or SSDI benefits to a very small amount, it is still worth applying, as establishing worthiness for these governmental programs may also confer eligibility for Medicare, Medicaid, food stamps, Department of Housing and Urban Development housing programs, vocational programs, and more. In some states, a separate application must be submitted for these programs, while in others, eligibility is conferred automatically.

Public Assistance

Public assistance, colloquially referred to as "welfare," is an underutilized source of potential income for qualifying patients with schizophrenia. Administered under the name "Temporary Assistance to Needy Families (TANF)," the program offers cash assistance to those who meet state-specific resource and income limitations. Though TANF funds are usually limited in duration to 2–5 years of benefits, patients and their relatives are encouraged to apply through their state's department of health and human services to determine potential eligibility, particularly in the case of sudden, illness-related job losses.

Food Stamps

Food stamps can be an important source of support for patients with schizophrenia, though this benefit often goes underutilized as well. Application for food stamps benefits can be made at your relative's local social services office and is based on his or her income in relation to the poverty line. The specific amount of benefits awarded varies by state and is based on both income levels and the cost of food. Benefit amounts may rise and fall depending on changes in the cost of food within the given region.

Veterans Benefits

If the patient was engaged in active military service at the onset of schizophrenia symptoms, he or she may be eligible for additional assistance from the Veterans Administration (VA). VA payments are especially worth pursuing, as they are often quite generous and may total more than $2,000/month when all available programs are taken into account. To check your relative's eligibility or apply for benefits, visit the Veterans Affairs website at http://www.benefits.va.gov/ or visit your regional VA office for assistance.

Housing

We are not far removed from the days when it was routine to send away all seriously ill patients to be institutionalized. However, today there are other options available for housing. If, for whatever reason, your relative is no longer able to live with you or independently, any of the following housing options may be practical alternatives:

Professional supervision. This category of housing options includes crisis houses, halfway houses, and quarter-way houses, all of which are staffed with trained personnel who are able to provide qualified support 24 hours a day.

Nonprofessional supervision. Another housing alternative includes foster homes, board-and-care homes, boarding houses, group homes, and congregate care homes, all of which have an untrained supervisor in residence all or part of the time.

Intermittent supervision. For patients who prefer a greater degree of independence, apartment buildings, hotels, and group homes exist in which patients are set up to live on their own, with support from a case manager or mental health professional who stops by periodically.

Determining the appropriate housing option for your relative can be challenging and may depend on your ability to provide caregiving support, the patient's financial resources, and the alternatives that are available in your community. Additional information on choosing and financing a housing option can be found in Appendix C, but bear in mind that the following factors are all considered to be common denominators of good housing programs:

Patients are treated with warmth and dignity. Unfortunately, there are rare situations in which housing sponsors have been charged with withholding support, stealing patient resources, or even using patients as a source of cheap labor. Observing the way caregivers treat their patients can give you important insight into the operations of each facility.

Facilities host a maximum of 15–20 people. Housing options that take on more patients than this are often pressed for resources and stretched too thin, inhibiting their ability to care for those in their charge.

Facilities serve as part of a continuum of care. As schizophrenia is a chronic condition, with symptom severity that can fluctuate over time, patients may need varying levels of support over time, from full-time assistance to minimal supervision.

Activities integrated with housing. There are housing options that combine lodging with social gatherings, therapy groups, and even employment opportunities. Such programs can improve patients' overall quality of life and offer a sense of community to schizophrenia sufferers.

Again, more information on this important subject is provided in Appendix C. Use these additional resources to learn more about the different housing options that may be available to you, as well as the governmental and charitable organizations that may offer assistance in paying for them.

EMPLOYMENT

For most adults, working is an important aspect of their lives. Beyond the financial security that a job offers, work is also important to maintain self-worth. Because schizophrenia typically strikes at a young age, before embarking on a career path, patients' efforts at employment get derailed. Thus, attempts at getting patients started on the employment path can be challenging. However, there are many programs that help patients develop job skills and find employment suitable to their particular level of functioning. One should be mindful, however, that some patients might never be able to work because of severity of the illness. Further, even those patients who are gainfully employed at the onset of their disease may find that symptom recurrence—as well as the side effects of prescription medications—makes them unable to maintain these positions in the long run.

Regardless, employment should be included in the recovery plan as a long-term goal. There are many benefits of the right type of work, including a boost in self-esteem, daily structure, a built-in social network, and an increased likelihood of treatment adherence in order to maintain employment. The following are common programs for full- or part-time employment, and alternative job programs:

Supported employment. In this environment, a patient selects the job of his or her choice and is given training and support both before the job begins and throughout the first few months of work.

Sheltered employment. These are jobs from which patients are not expected to progress to competitive employment, such as job opportunities provided by Goodwill Industries.

Transitional employment. In transitional employment programs, patients are given jobs to which a rehabilitation specialist accompanies them until they are able to do the work themselves. Alternatively, they may split the work with another patient so that two patients share responsibility for a single shift until *graduation*.

Job skills training. These programs help patients develop the skills needed for traditional employment.

HEALTH SYSTEM CHALLENGES

Beyond the issue of good access to healthcare is the issue of negotiating complex health systems. If you are receiving care in a large hospital organization, then you need to be able to interact effectively with parts that are relevant to psychiatric care, including emergency services, inpatient facilities, outpatient clinics, medical services, rehabilitation, day programs, and so on. It can be frustrating trying to line up all the needed services, making appointments with the right people, finding these places, affording transportation, finding parking, and so on. Fortunately, your primary point of contact—the care team—should be able to guide you through different parts of the medical system as needs arise. Be aware, however, there are several other reasons that can add to frustrations:

Limited health provider resources. It is common to find that hospitals lack inpatient beds for mental health services, lack experts for schizophrenia treatment, as well as having available appointments within a reasonable amount of time.

Inferior care. Care team members try to do the best under the circumstances in which they function. However, there are many reasons why you may not be getting optimal care, including communication failures, inadequate follow-up, inadequate or unavailable therapeutic programming, or overburdened staff. If these issues are not addressable, then you need to consider alternative care settings, if this is feasible.

Continuity of treatment. Turnover of staff is an unfortunate reality of modern medical systems, and this can be especially difficult if the patient forges a special bond with a provider who ultimately leaves. Under the best of circumstances, transfers of care should be planned and seamless.

Insurance coverage limitations/restrictions. If enrolled in a private insurance program, you may find yourself hindered by coverage limitations (e.g., the number of days of covered inpatient or outpatient treatment), medications that fall outside of the approved formulary or restrictions in the practitioners who can be accessed. Your care team can try to directly address some concerns with the insurance company, but be warned that it may not always be successful. Changing insurances may solve some limitations, but may introduce other limitations. Fortunately, care teams are familiar with these problems, and will try to provide the best care possible within these limits.

The passage of the Affordable Care Act makes it illegal for insurers to charge mental health patients more or to deny them coverage based on preexisting conditions, as of 2014.

SUMMARY

- There are a variety of symptom-related, behavioral (low socialization, drug abuse) and structural (finances, housing) challenges that emerge as a consequence of schizophrenia.
- Early recognition of these problems and anticipating potential issues before they become emergencies can minimize the negative consequences.
- Experiencing stress in situations that may not seem stressful to others is relatively common. Decreasing stress by developing daily routines and other stress reduction techniques is valuable in maintaining stability.
- Due to schizophrenia, there is shrinking of the social network, the reasons for which include communication problems, loss of social skills, symptoms, and stigma. Teaching new communication skills and offering social skills training can reduce these complications.

- Drug and alcohol abuse pose a significant risk to symptom relapse. Keeping an eye out for warning signs and taking immediate action when abuse is suspected can help minimize this serious issue.
- Several financial support options exist to help patients with schizophrenia in the event that your personal finances are insufficient. SSI, SSDI, public assistance, food stamps, and veterans' benefits (if eligible) are all potential sources of income.
- If your relative is no longer able to live independently or in your home, housing programs that provide professional supervision, nonprofessional or intermittent supervision exist. Program availability is location-dependent and may be paid for with public or personal funds.
- Schizophrenia patients who worked before their diagnoses are more likely to maintain employment after it. Patients who are interested in and able to work may benefit from supported, sheltered, or transitional employment programs.
- Navigating the health system can be challenging, and schizophrenia patients may run into issues of limited resources, suboptimal care, care team continuity, and insurance coverage limitations. Make sure your care team will work to address such roadblocks to your care.

CHAPTER 16

Managing Crises

Losing your head in a crisis is a good way to become the crisis.
C. J. REDWINE, *DEFIANCE*

Despite the very best care offered and the best caregiving, crises—minor or major ones—are a fact of life with schizophrenia. Crises can be relatively minor (poor sleep leading to worsening symptoms) or true emergencies (violence toward others or self). Although such crises can be frightening, having the skills to handle them effectively and in a timely manner can mean the difference between a situation that's defused quickly and one that spirals out of control.

In this chapter, we review common situations that can be troublesome and, if unaddressed, become crises. Therefore, some degree of vigilance is always required to detect impending trouble. Better still is to have a plan in place if a crisis is brewing (contact information, hospital locations, and other emergency support resources).

Most crises emerge from a worsening of positive symptoms, such as delusions, hallucinations, and thought disturbance. Occasionally, severe negative symptoms, such as apathy, can lead to extreme self-neglect (not eating or cleaning self). Such clinical worsening can be due to variety of reasons—treatment failure, treatment nonadherence, substance abuse, medical issues, interpersonal issues, losses of people and places.

In most instances, clinical worsening happens over a period of days; rarely is it instantaneous. There are generally two phases of clinical worsening:

Decompensation. This is clinical worsening from a current level of stability. The severity of this state can wax and wane. The clinical state can spontaneously return to the previous level of stability without requiring any changes in treatment. However, if the

Defusing Crises

If you or someone else in the family is confronting a behavioral crisis, keep the following in mind to defuse the situation sufficiently until professional help can be reached:

Maintain a calm demeanor. No matter how angry or belligerent your relative becomes, yelling and shouting yourself won't help the situation. Staying calm in the midst of a crisis is incredibly difficult, but it is important to prevent your emotions and anxiety from taking control.

Acknowledge feelings. Do not tell your relative that there is nothing to worry about. In his mind, the situation very much warrants his current behavior! Instead, acknowledge what he may be feeling, and remind him that you're there to support him with whatever he's going through.

Avoid continuous eye contact, finger pointing, and critical remarks. Prolonged eye contact may seem threatening, while finger pointing and critical marks can make patients feel judged and attacked. When interacting with a patient who is experiencing a crisis, speak in a normal tone, and minimize excess body movements in order to create a calming presence.

Comply with safe and reasonable requests. If your relative is experiencing delusions or hallucinations, it can be helpful to go along with requests that you can fulfill in a reasonable manner until help arrives. If, for example, she asks for assistance putting tin foil on the windows to help block radio signals from being transmitted to her brain, doing so puts nobody at risk and may help the patient to calm down enough to defuse the crisis.

Take threats seriously. Threats of physical violence or self-harm should not be dismissed as simple symptoms of the crisis. If your relative makes threats against you, acknowledge that you feel your safety has been compromised and take necessary steps to keep yourself safe.

clinical state continues to decline, it can lead to a full-blown state of relapse.

Relapse. Although there are a variety of research benchmarks for relapse, in general it is understood as clinical worsening that requires active intervention that could be a simple adjustment of APD dose to requiring hospitalization.

RECOGNIZING CRISES

Crises in the context of schizophrenia come in all "shapes and sizes." Recognizing signs that may indicate an impending crisis will permit getting timely help. Some behaviors that are worrisome include the following:

- Increasingly hypervigilant or suspicious of others' intentions
- Hearing voices that are more threatening than usual or that seem to provoke dangerous actions
- Sudden (or worsening) fear that someone wants to hurt him or her
- Increasing agitation and incessant pacing
- Worsening speech (indicative of worsening thought disorder)

Additional signs of worsening include the following:

- Becoming increasingly socially withdrawn
- Losing interest in eating or eating excessively
- No longer performing routine self-care or daily activities
- Spending much more time asleep
- Mood worsens or fluctuates between extremes
- Suicidal thoughts or actions

Any patient experiencing an acute crisis or a more gradual decline is unlikely to experience all of these symptoms at once. Therefore, it is important to monitor your relative's condition and report any changes or out-of-the-ordinary behaviors to your care team for review.

CONSIDERING HOSPITALIZATION

Your care team can give you a number of different options for managing a developing or ongoing crisis, including hospitalization. For instance, if the situation is not severe, your clinicians or emergency contacts may suggest a medication or dosage change, or a private office visit. More urgent situations, however, may require assessment in an emergency department and subsequent admission to a psychiatric hospital (or a general hospital with psychiatric beds). The patient may go to the emergency department on his or her own, or be transported by relatives or friends. In most extreme situations, public emergency systems may need to be activated (e.g., police, ambulance).

Hospitalization may be required to:

- Manage a suicide attempt
- Prevent imminent self-harm or harm to others

- Detoxify from alcohol or other drug abuse
- Manage serious medical issues
- Oversee complicated medication changes
- Provide close ongoing observation not possible outside the hospital setting

However, hospitalization is always the last resort. If a psychiatric evaluation establishes that a lower level of care (step-down care) can safely address the crisis, alternative treatment settings may be utilized, such as mobile outreach teams, ACT programs, crisis housing, partial hospitalization, or assisted outpatient treatment (AOT), also called outpatient commitment.

If the decision is made to hospitalize your relative, ask if a scheduled admission is available, as this will prevent you from having to wait in the chaotic emergency room. In either case, have available as much information about current and past treatments (particularly when dealing with a new clinical setting) in order to expedite the admission process. You may also find it helpful to familiarize yourself with the commitment laws in your state, as these regulations may affect whether the patient can be hospitalized without his or her consent, how long he or she can be detained involuntarily, and what to do in the event of an emergency.

WORKING WITH LAW ENFORCEMENT

Sometimes, the first responders in an emergency are the police. Common situations for which police get called are suicidal behaviors, threatening others, being assaultive, wielding a weapon or other threatening behaviors, disturbing the peace, and bizarre public behaviors.

In recent years, many law enforcement agencies have undergone extensive mental health response training and therefore are better able to support the community during psychiatric crises. However, there are situations in which the psychiatrically disturbed patient is taken first to police detention, rather than a hospital. If this has happened before, you may find it helpful to reach out to your local law enforcement departments and alert them (in general terms) about your or your relative's needs. Doing so will help police respond appropriately; this will mean receiving timely and appropriate care.

Handling an Arrest

There may be situations that result in you or your relative being arrested. It is important to inform the police, at the earliest opportunity, that the more appropriate resolution to the current issue may be a psychiatric evaluation. Depending on the circumstances, transfer to a mental health facility may happen speedily. If detention is going to occur, the following suggestions may be helpful:

Explain the patient's mental health history to the officer (if he or she is not already familiar with your relative's case). Depending on the severity of the alleged crime, the officer may be able to help you get emergency psychiatric care instead of arrest. The officer may also be willing to drop or modify any charges.

Alert the care team. Many care teams have liaisons with police departments; they may be able to effect transfer to psychiatric hospital or at the least ensure ongoing psychiatric care while in detention or jail.

Be proactive during arraignment hearings. If you are not able to get your relative released pre-trial (or, better yet, have his or her case diverted to a mental health court, if these are available in your state), do your best to attend any arraignment hearings that occur and ensure the defense attorney has all the facts at hand.

Ensure the patient's safety. The more awareness the judicial system has about you or your relative's psychiatric needs, the more likely it is to receive appropriate supervision while in detention, hence greater safety for everyone. It may be appropriate to inform jail staff about suicidal risk, which is greater during the first 1–2 days of incarceration. Explain to the mental health professionals working at the jail that you are concerned for your relative's safety and ask what can be done to improve his safety while jailed. Planning for release is another important consideration, as having the appropriate services lined up for your relative in advance will make the transition much smoother.

You may also find yourself working with law enforcement in the unfortunate event that your relative goes missing. Even if the police have been alerted, you'll want to take action on your own. Being very mindful of privacy issues, you may want to recruit friends and family in the search of places he or she is known to frequent. The use of social networks (Facebook and Twitter) may be helpful, but it may needlessly risk the patient being "exposed" and be subjected to even more stigma. For further information on handling your relative's legal issues or disappearance, the National Alliance on Mental Illness can be a great resource and can be reached at 800–950–6264 or http://www.nami.org/.

"PREVENTING" CRISES

As Benjamin Franklin wisely said, "An ounce of prevention is worth a pound of cure." This particularly is the case with schizophrenia, because it is a lifelong illness and the likelihood of at least one crisis occurring is quite high. While there is no certain way of preventing a crisis, there are many commonsense and patient-specific strategies that can decrease the risk. This usually means educating yourself about risk factors for decompensation/relapse, and attending to them if they emerge. In Figure 16.1, you can see how a variety of factors can contribute to decompensation.

Most of these risk factors have been discussed in different sections of the book, but here we provide a very brief overview:

> **Stress.** Worsening symptoms are often a result of stress. Therefore, strategies to minimize stress are important in maintaining clinical stability.

> **Treatment nonadherence.** As we have repeatedly stressed, stopping treatment or not following proper medication regimen is one of the commonest reasons for relapse, and underlies many crises.

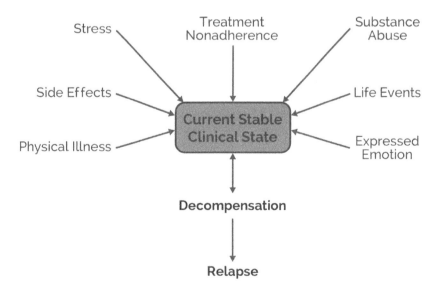

Figure 16.1 Factors Associated with Relapse

Substance abuse. Abuse of alcohol, marijuana, or other drugs, before or after the onset of schizophrenia, is very common (at least 50% use). Substance abuse or dependence is associated with poorer treatment outcome, including hospitalizations.

Side effects. Certain side effects of APDs or other medications can cause physical and psychological distress (e.g., akathisia) that can result in agitated states or discontinuation of medication.

Physical illnesses. Worsening of coexisting medical conditions (e.g., seizures or diabetes), or a new medical issue, can precipitate decompensation.

Treatment failure. Occasionally, medications that once worked can become less effective without forewarning. There are many reasons why this may occur (change in health status, drug interactions with a new medication, increased smoking), requiring either dosage adjustment or a new treatment plan entirely.

Adverse life events. Any major change—positive or negative—in our lives can be stressful. In the case of patients with schizophrenia, such changes can result in clinical worsening that need to be addressed promptly. Issues that commonly seem to result in greater stress are losses (parents, caregivers, care team, or friends moving away) as well as new circumstances (new relationships, graduating from a supervised setting, new work setting). Seemingly benign life events, such as having to go to a new pharmacy, can be stressful and shouldn't be ignored.

Expressed emotion (EE). The attitudes expressed verbally or nonverbally, toward the patient by the caregiver or within the family, are known as expressed emotion (EE). These can be negative (critical comments, hostility, anger, rejecting, ignoring, blaming, negligence) or positive (warm comments) *High* EE refers to a negative communication style, and is associated with higher hospitalization rates. In other words, hostility and negative comments by caregivers or other members of the family can lead to worsening symptoms and poorer treatment outcome.

Another component of high EE is *emotional over-involvement.* Here the caregivers, usually mothers, are overprotective of patients, excessively concerned for them, blaming themselves, neglecting their own personal needs, and sacrificing in other ways. This has a negative effect on the patient in terms of fostering dependence, preventing personal growth and self-reliance, thus, impeding recovery. Paradoxically, this leads to anxiety on part of the patient who now has concerns about having future caregiving.

Low EE, on the other hand, is communication that is infused with positive regard, encouragement, kindness, and empathy. This form of communication includes genuine smiling, as well as demonstrating affection to the extent it is tolerated by the patient. Low EE is focused less on symptoms and behavior and more on positive aspects of the person. Appreciation of patient's "good" behavior should be verbalized. This is not to say that unacceptable behaviors should be accepted; rather, limits should be set in a non-blaming manner.

Identify Crisis Resources in Advance

Should a crisis occur, having critical pieces of information on hand can make the situation much more manageable. Do not assume that you will be near your preferred hospital or able to access your current care team. Quite possibly you may need to review your relative's condition with a new set of professionals.

Therefore, it is best to be prepared by having the following information readily available (see Appendix D for form that may be useful):

- The names, roles, and contact information of all current members of your care team
- Phone numbers and addresses of:
  - Emergency rooms, psychiatric hospitals, or other mental health facilities in your area (or any area where your relative are traveling to)
  - Mobile outreach teams, crisis response teams, and assertive community treatment (ACT) programs
  - Name and contact information of your pharmacy
  - Friends or family members who are familiar with your relative's condition
  - Police stations near you, as well as the names and phone numbers of any law enforcement members who are aware of your relative's condition
- A list of the diagnoses, current medications with dosages and frequency
- A list of any past medications, as well as the reasons for their discontinuation, particularly if any serious side effects were encountered
- Current alcohol or drug abuse, if present

If you are the patient or a caregiver, it is highly recommended that this information is stored in a safe, yet easily accessible, place that is also private. If you decide to have this information stored on a home computer, or other sites (e.g., cloud storage) it is imperative that there is good data security. No matter how you choose to store your information, be sure to update it regularly, particularly when there are significant changes in treatment or medical status. Out-of-date information may just add further confusion to an already tense situation.

SUMMARY

- Schizophrenia is a lifelong illness that can have periods of symptomatic worsening—decompensation—that may reach crisis proportions.
- Crises may come on rather suddenly or may be the result of a downward spiral. Recognizing the signs and symptoms associated with impending crises gives you time to get help. Contact the care team or activate emergency services as the situation dictates.
- Hospitalization may be necessary to address a relapse, but it is not the only option. Intensive outpatient treatment, mobile outreach teams, crisis response teams, and assertive community treatment (ACT) programs may be reasonable alternatives.
- Law enforcement may become involved in managing the crisis if imminent or active danger exists to the patient, you, or others. Work with law enforcement officers to ensure patient's safety, whether he or she is released, arrested, held pending trial, or jailed.
- There are a number of known factors that increase the risk of a relapse, and addressing them proactively can substantially reduce the odds of a crisis.
- If you are in the middle of a crisis, it may be possible to defuse it by maintaining a calm demeanor, acknowledging your relative's feelings, avoiding threatening behaviors, and complying with safe and reasonable requests. If the patient makes threats against your safety, take them very seriously.
- Advance preparation for managing a crisis will be very valuable to the patient, caregiver, first responders, and treatment providers. Such preparation is relatively easy to accomplish by keeping up-to-date records of diagnoses, medications, and other pertinent information. These records should be stored in a safe, accessible, and private place.

Science of Schizophrenia

Biological Foundations of Schizophrenia

What Does the Future Hold?

CHAPTER 17

Biological Foundations of Schizophrenia

> The ever quickening advances of science made possible by the success of the Human Genome Project will also soon let us . . . seek out appropriate therapies for such illnesses as schizophrenia and bipolar disease.
> JAMES D. WATSON, NOBEL PRIZE WINNER FOR DISCOVERING DNA

The information presented in this chapter is a *tiny tip of the iceberg* that represents a vast amount of research observations that have accumulated in recent decades. There are many fields of study within the broad scope of neuroscience, each of which provides a piece of the puzzle. While we have some ways to go before the puzzle is completed, we are beginning to understand its general shape. With that in mind, the next few pages provide some information and terms that you are likely to come across in your own readings and discussions about schizophrenia.

CAUSES OF SCHIZOPHRENIA

Since the earliest days of recognizing schizophrenia as a separate condition from other psychiatric disorders, there has been intense search for its cause; in the beginning there were few clues. Eugen Bleuler, the psychiatrist who gave us the name schizophrenia, noted a century ago that relatives of patients with schizophrenia were often "tainted by hereditary mental disease." This has led to such questions as, does it run in families, or is it genetic, or is it both? If it is genetic, what are the genes involved and how does that result in schizophrenia, as we know it? There are many details about the causes of schizophrenia that have yet to be uncovered. However, there has been a great deal of progress that is enabling us to narrow the questions, which have led to better clues about where in the brain we should be looking more closely.

To be fair, there has been a minority of psychiatrists, primarily Dr. Thomas Szasz, who have argued that schizophrenia is not a disease at all, but a myth and a moral problem! In response, a well-known psychiatrist and researcher Dr. Seymour Kety responded, "If schizophrenia is a myth, it is a genetically transmitted myth!" Practically no clinician or researcher anymore believes that schizophrenia is anything other than a brain disorder.

It is currently believed that schizophrenia is not a disorder brought about by to a *single* cause. It is also likely that there are different forms of the condition, which complicates the search for causes. There is evidence that suggests both genes (*nature*) and environment (*nurture*) have a role, referred to as *gene-environment interaction*. There has been an enormous amount of research conducted in the past hundred years, into practically every aspect of schizophrenia. It is impossible to summarize it in a short amount of space. However, we review here *very* briefly the current scientific focus and thinking about schizophrenia.

Is Schizophrenia Familial?

Given the early observations that there was increased occurrence of schizophrenia in close relatives of patients, some of the earliest research studies examined this issue. What was discovered is that the chance of developing schizophrenia in a person increases the closer their relationship is with a relative who already has schizophrenia (see Figure 17.1.). For example, the chances of developing schizophrenia is highest (nearly 50%) when an identical twin has schizophrenia, or if both parents have it. Brother and sisters have much less of a risk (about 10%). Cousins, aunts, and uncles have even less of a risk (2%). While the risk is very low when there is no family history of schizophrenia, the risk is never zero. What this evidence points to is that *heritability* is a major risk factor. However, just as importantly, what the evidence shows is that heritability does not explain everything. After all, if the risk is only 50% in *identical* twins, who presumably have nearly the same genes, the other 50% risk has to be explained. Therefore, there have to be other factors—environmental (i.e., not genetic) or developmental (growth-related)—that account for this discrepancy.

How Is Schizophrenia Transmitted?

Although we now accept that there is a genetic factor operating in schizophrenia, the specific method of this transmission (passing on) remains unclear. Current evidence indicates that a complex process is ongoing, with many genes involved and multiple other factors interacting or

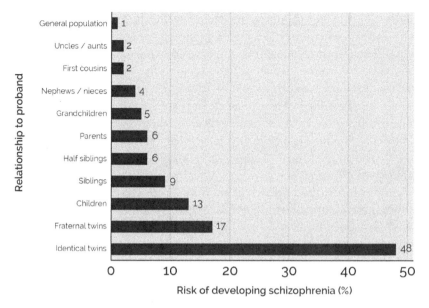

Figure 17.1 Risk of Developing Schizophrenia (from Gottesman, 1991)

influencing each other, to result in schizophrenia (*multifactorial/poly-genic model*) (Figure 17.2).

What Is Transmitted?

Another way of thinking about genetic risk is to ask the question, what is actually transmitted (passed on)? The notion is that the signs and symptoms, which we recognize as schizophrenia, may only be the tip of the iceberg; in fact, many more people in the general population probably have a *liability* (increased risk) for developing the illness. This risk may express itself as poor psychosocial functioning, oddness, or other types of psychoses, but that they never go on to develop schizophrenia. In other words, some people with liability for schizophrenia go on to develop the condition, others develop conditions along the lines of schizophrenia called *schizophrenia spectrum disorders* (e.g., schizotypal personality disorder), and some do not show any such signs. This observation has led to the search for genes that are involved in schizophrenia.

The Search for Schizophrenia Genes

Molecular genetics is a scientific discipline that studies the structure and function of genes at the very fine level. In other words, what do genes actually do? But before one can determine the function of genes, one has to find out where they are, and which ones are important for schizophrenia. Each of these questions is answered by using a variety of highly specialized, labor-intensive laboratory techniques. Beyond this are questions about what genes produce, how they interact with other genes, and whether we can influence the outcome of these genetic processes in order to ultimately better treat, or even prevent, schizophrenia. We are quite far from that point. However, as a patient or relative, it is important to be aware that a great deal of research is ongoing to improve the lives of patients in the future.

In terms of identifying which genes may be related to schizophrenia, a sophisticated scientific technique called *genome-wide association studies* (GWAS) has been used, in which variations within a particular gene are examined, and whether these genes are likely to have a small or large effect for the specific condition. In one massive study involving over a 150,000 people, 108 gene locations were identified as important. Many

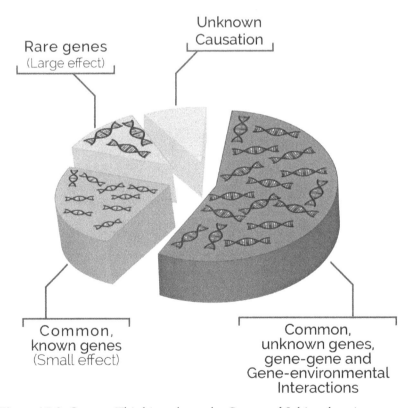

Figure 17.2 Current Thinking about the Causes of Schizophrenia

studies have revealed that there are multiple common genes with a small effect, accounting for a large proportion of the heritability of schizophrenia. Other studies have revealed rare genetic mutations with a large effect. One way to understand all this confusing research is to imagine how big a slice of a pie is for each assumption about the genetics of schizophrenia (Figure 17.2).

Environmental Factors

As noted earlier, genes have a prominent but not exclusive role in the development of schizophrenia. There are several biological and psychosocial environmental factors that have been found to be associated with risk for schizophrenia, as discussed in detail earlier in this book (Chapter 4: Who Gets Schizophrenia?). These factors are:

- **Perinatal (around birth) complications.** These increase risk of subtle brain injury.
- **Paternal age.** There is evidence that the risk of developing schizophrenia is about three times higher if a child's father is over the age of 50 at his or her birth, compared with children whose fathers are under the age of 30.
- **Season of birth.** Those born in winter/early spring may be at a slightly increased risk for schizophrenia.
- **Being born in urban areas.** There is evidence that schizophrenia is slightly more common in those born in inner-city neighborhoods.

How do environmental factors influence gene function? It has been said that while we are born with the book of life (the genetic blueprint), what determines how this blueprint is expressed is determined by which pages of this book are opened! Environmental factors can influence whether a gene is expressed or not by acting on certain chemical modifications (e.g., methylation) without actually changing the genetic code. These influences, collectively, are called *epigenetics*. Many scientists believe that at least some of the clinical expression of schizophrenia may be related to epigenetic modifications of the genome by environmental factors.

BRAIN MECHANISMS UNDERLYING SCHIZOPHRENIA

Despite a century of research, we have only a vague understanding of what goes wrong with the brain in schizophrenia. However, much has been learned about *what* goes wrong with brain structure, function, and brain chemistry in schizophrenia, and *how* such abnormalities may be caused during development.

Neuroanatomical Alterations

It has long been recognized that there are neuroanatomical (brain structure) alterations, but precisely what these were could be discovered only after there were advances in techniques to study the living brain. For example, CT studies show that cerebral ventricles (spaces in the brain that are filled with a special fluid) are enlarged, suggesting a reduction in brain tissue (Figure 17.3). These findings, as well those from studies using other brain imaging techniques, have helped firmly establish that schizophrenia is a disease of the brain.

Brain imaging research has described a large variety of physical brain abnormalities, such as:

- Reduced brain volume (amount of space taken up by something) between 5% and 10%, especially in *gray matter* (so called because this brain tissue is grayish in color, and contains many different types of nerve cells; white matter, on the other hand, largely contains nerve fibers)
- Enlarged lateral and third ventricles
- Decreased volume of the specific brain areas (superior temporal gyri and medial temporal cortex, particularly the hippocampus and amygdala)

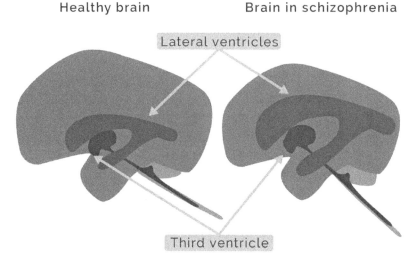

Figure 17.3 Ventricle Enlargement and Brain Atrophy in Schizophrenia

- Subtle reductions in the volume of the prefrontal cortex (front part of the brain that is associated with decision making, planning, social behavior)
- Reductions in the size of the corpus callosum (a broad white matter band of nerve fibers joining the two halves of the brain, and allows the two sides to communicate)

Brain changes appear to be present at the onset of the illness. These changes are more severe the longer the duration of untreated psychosis. There also is an indication that there are continued brain changes after the onset of psychosis. Studies that have followed patients with an first episode over a number of years have shown gray matter losses during the first few years of the illness. Based on such findings, it has been suggested that some brain changes may progress, at least during the early years in the course of schizophrenia. If this is true, early interventions with medications and/or psychotherapy may halt the progress of brain abnormalities in schizophrenia, and result in a better clinical outcome.

Since subtle psychotic-like symptoms and social withdrawal (the prodromal phase) occur quite frequently before the first episode of schizophrenia, one wonders whether the physical brain changes happen alongside the behavioral decline during this period. If true, this further strengthens the connection between brain alterations and schizophrenia.

Another question to ask about brain changes and schizophrenia is whether persons who are at a high risk of developing this disorder already show brain alterations before *any* indications of schizophrenia. What has been found is that individuals at high genetic risk have reduced brain volume in very specific brain areas (amygdala-hippocampal and thalamus). Very recently, Dr. Tyrone Cannon and his colleagues concluded a large research study that showed gray matter volume reductions occuring in patients in the prodromal phase of schizophrenia, during follow-up, particularly in those who go on to develop psychotic episodes. This is very suggestive that an active disordered brain process is taking place during the *transition* from prodrome to psychosis.

Neurochemical Alterations

More than a hundred neurotransmitters (chemical messengers produced by brain cells) have been identified so far. However, a relatively small number of these are thought to have a primary role in schizophrenia, particularly dopamine, but some others as well. It is also possible that more fundamental defects, perhaps in the membranes (walls) of brain cells, may also be involved. For each of these alternative propositions there are varying degrees of evidence available.

Dopamine. Dopamine (DA) is a neurotransmitter that is active in many areas of the brain believed to be involved in schizophrenia. For example, in the higher cerebral cortex, DA is important for cognitive function (thinking, reasoning, judgment). In lower brain regions such as the limbic system, dopamine is important for reward and risk taking, and for attaching meaning to experience. The conventional assumption over the past 50 years has been that psychotic symptoms are related to excess of dopamine in the limbic system. In support of this view is the fact that all effective antipsychotics block dopamine (Figure 17.4), and the fact that drugs such as amphetamine and cocaine increase dopamine levels, and can cause psychotic symptoms. Direct evidence for the dopamine hypothesis, however, has been lacking. This includes the observation that levels of homovanillic acid, a breakdown product of dopamine, are increased in the cerebrospinal fluid of patients with schizophrenia.

The classic dopamine theory

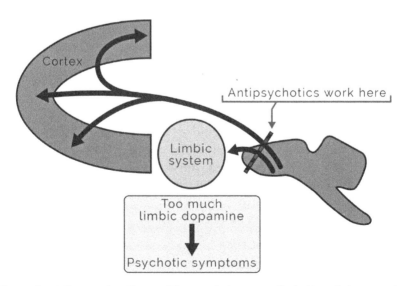

Figure 17.4 Dopamine Excess Theory. It is generally believed that psychosis is related to an excess of neurotransmitter release by the dopaminergic neurons.

A more refined theory of dopamine abnormality has been proposed by Dr. Daniel Weinberger, in which he proposed that the positive symptoms (psychosis) may be related to increased dopamine activity in the limbic system, and that the negative and cognitive symptoms in schizophrenia may be related to decreased dopamine activity in the cortical system (Figure 17.5).

Gamma amino butyric acid (GABA) and glutamate. GABA and glutamate are interconnected neurotransmitters. GABA is an inhibitory neurotransmitter (reduces certain cell functions), while glutamate is excitatory (increases function). A balance between the two is necessary for normal brain activity, and when the balance is off, a psychiatric disorder may be the result. We know that GABA controls the amount of DA released by the brain cells. It has been discovered that there is loss of a type of GABA neuron in parts of the brain that are implicated in schizophrenia (hippocampus and cingulate), which very well could explain the excess amount of DA found in schizophrenia.

Glutamate is the most plentiful neurotransmitter in the brain. Magnetic resonance spectroscopy (MRS) studies suggest changes in glutamate levels in schizophrenia. Such alterations may lead to abnormal DA responses to stress, which predisposes to psychotic symptoms. It is noteworthy that the drug phencyclidine (PCP), which blocks glutamate

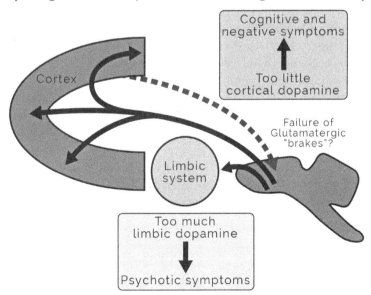

Figure 17.5 The Revised Dopamine Hypothesis of Schizophrenia

receptors (regions in the cell that respond to a specific neurotransmitters), can cause symptoms similar to schizophrenia.

Other neurotransmitter systems. Two other neurotransmitters have been studied more intensively. One of them is *serotonin*; it became interesting because lysergic acid diethylamide (LSD), which can result in psychosis, binds to the serotonin receptor. Also, the effectiveness of the APD clozapine is related to its effect on serotonin. There is some evidence that increased activity of the neurotransmitter *noradrenaline* may also be involved in schizophrenia. However, the overall evidence proclaiming the large role serotonin and noradrenaline have in the causation of schizophrenia is weak.

Cell membrane alterations and oxidative stress. It has been suggested that alterations in structure and function of brain cell membranes (walls) may occur in schizophrenia, and that such defects may explain the changed functioning of receptors and neurotransmitter that repeatedly have been observed. The actual evidence, however, has mostly been indirect. Nevertheless, it is an interesting area of research, partly because cell membranes are made up of a variety of chemical compounds, including the well-known omega-3 fatty acids. There is some evidence that taking omega-3 fatty acids (contained in fish oil) may potentially reverse such membrane defects, and improve some symptoms. However, the research evidence is not enough to recommend fish oil as a routine treatment.

Another interesting notion is that free radicals and antioxidants are involved in schizophrenia. Free radicals are natural chemicals all over the body and, when produced in excess (*oxidative stress*), can harm the cells membrane. There is a decent amount of evidence that such oxidative stress is occurring in schizophrenia. The body also has very complex chemical systems, with hundreds of different chemicals, to counteract free radicals (antioxidants). Some familiar antioxidants are vitamins C and E, glutathione, and coenzyme Q. Then there are important antioxidant enzymes such as superoxide dismutase, glutathione peroxidase, and catalase. Researchers are studying whether such oxidative stress may have a role in schizophrenia; there is a broad variety of evidence to show that this is the case (Figure 17.6). However, so far, good quality evidence that antioxidant supplements have therapeutic benefits is minor.

Another avenue of research in recent years has been the area of inflammation, which is the body's complex response to cell damage involving a cascade of chemicals. In schizophrenia, there is accumulating evidence that inflammatory processes may contribute to its risk. What researchers have shown is that blood levels of certain inflammatory

Oxidative stress, inflammation and schizophrenia

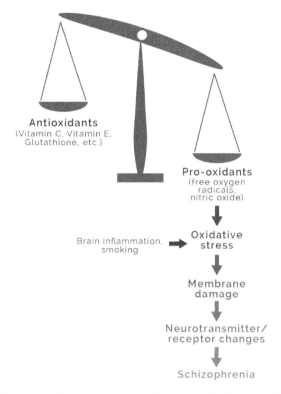

Figure 17.6 Oxidative Stress Pathways That May Be Involved in Cell Membrane Damage

factors (e.g., interleukins) are increased in schizophrenia, and that anti-inflammatory medicines such as aspirin and minocycline may be of therapeutic value. Much more research is needed, however, to confirm such observations.

When Might the (Biological) Disorder Really Begin?

We are familiar with the notion of "onset of illness'" which generally refers to the onset of clinical manifestations which we recognize as schizophrenia. However, that doesn't tell us what biological events may be going on in the brain, and when these might be occurring. For example, could schizophrenia begin in the womb, but expresses itself clinically 15–20 years later? Or, is it that the risk for schizophrenia preexists but the neurobiological events occur in adolescence, shortly before the symptoms become apparent? Answers to these questions, also referred

to as *neurodevelopmental models*, are vital to developing early management approaches to reducing the severity of the illness, and perhaps even
prevent it from emerging.

There are two theories that offer an explanation for the clinical observations. One is called the *early developmental model*, which proposes
the occurrence of subtle brain development problems around or before
birth, and thus leads to improper brain development in early adulthood.
There is little direct evidence for this model, but there are plenty of hints
that this is occurring based on a variety of observations in patients. For
example, in children at risk for schizophrenia, there is an increased rate
of birth complications; there are subtle neurological signs and behavioral abnormalities. These are known as *risk indicators*.

The "late" neuro developmental model proposes that brain changes
underlying schizophrenia occur just before the onset of psychosis, typically in late adolescence. Normally, during adolescence there occurs a
process in the brain during which there is a fine-tuning of nerve cell
connections; this involves the removal of *extra* synapses (a space where
nerve cells communicate with each other) that are no longer required.
The brain naturally weeds out the extra synapses by a process referred
to as *pruning*. However, if this pruning is excessive, then there is much
greater loss of synapses than should occur under normal circumstances,
setting the stage for brain impairment, and ultimately schizophrenia.
This idea is in line with the observation that at least a subgroup of

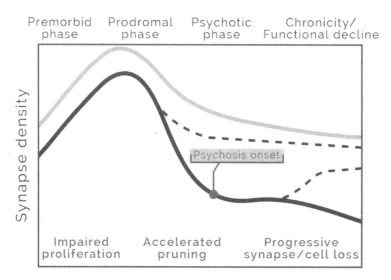

Figure 17.7 Developmental and Progressive Models of Schizophrenia

patients show progressive functional decline over the first few years of the illness.

These two neurodevelopmental models (Figure 17.7) are not necessarily mutually exclusive. It is quite possible that both processes can coexist, but the timing of each is different. Thus, it is possible that the first set of brain development problems (early developmental model) is followed by the next set of problems (late developmental model), leading to successive "hits" on the brain, resulting in illness. There may also be environmental factors that serve as triggers to these abnormal neurodevelopmental models, such as illicit drug use and psychosocial stresses.

SUMMARY

- Intensive research has been ongoing for many decades to decipher the causes of schizophrenia.
- Schizophrenia is highly heritable, with nearly 70% of its causal factors being explained by genetic inheritance.
- A large number of genes with small effect and a small number of genes with larger effect may account for the genetic causation of schizophrenia.
- Several environmental factors such as viral exposure, perinatal complications and childhood trauma may contribute to the risk for schizophrenia. Gene-environmental interactions are very likely to play a role.
- Neurotransmitter alterations, primarily dopamine, may underlie the biological underpinnings of psychosis. All currently available antipsychotic medications affect the dopamine system.
- Neurodevelopmental theories have been postulated to explain the age of onset of schizophrenia, in late teens and early adulthood, in relation to brain changes that may be occurring much earlier.

CHAPTER 18

What Does the Future Hold?

The future starts today, not tomorrow.

POPE JOHN PAUL II

There is always a future! It is understandable, however, for those suffering from schizophrenia today, and families dealing with this illness moment-to-moment, that thinking about future scientific and treatment advances may seem like a luxury. Nonetheless, being aware of these advances can give hope, as well motivation to hang in! Such awareness may even motivate you or your family to participate in research projects, thus actively helping knowledge move forward.

Here, we share some ideas and some promising directions that the field of schizophrenia research is taking. First, the neurobiological basis of schizophrenia is increasingly better understood as a result of sophisticated brain imaging techniques. These investigations are making it possible to characterize the brain structural and functional "signatures" of schizophrenia, which will then be easier to make the connections between these brain findings to the underlying genes. Second, the genes involved in schizophrenia are beginning to be identified; a recent important study revealed 108 gene variations related to schizophrenia.

However, research is also showing that neurobiology and genes do not exactly correspond to the diagnostic borders that are currently in use. Rather, this research will need to move toward biologically based definitions, rather than clinical diagnoses alone. This is important because clinical diagnosis alone is somewhat undependable in terms of guiding research into causes of a complex disorder that is schizophrenia. Using biologically based diagnostic criteria, on the other hand, will make it possible to identify new treatment targets, thus facilitating rapid identification of drugs to be tested in clinical trials. One such research initiative has been taken by the National Institute of Mental Health (NIMH), called the Research Domain Criteria (R-DoC), which is looking at ways to classify psychiatric disorders based on molecular, cellular, and brain circuitry information.

NEW DIRECTIONS AND INITIATIVE IN THE NEUROBIOLOGY OF PSYCHOTIC DISORDERS

Research into the neurobiology of psychoses has not revealed any single brain region, or any one kind of neurochemical dysfunction. This is because most psychiatric disorders, unlike many neurological illnesses, stem from widespread dysfunctions in multiple interconnected neural circuits, and from multiple neurochemical systems gone wrong. For these reasons, it is better to think of these disorders from a *systems* neuroscience perspective, that is, in terms of altered functioning and organization of brain circuits. The human brain is extraordinarily complex, with over one hundred *billion* neurons and a hundred *trillion* connections between nerve cells. The whole, complex mass of connections is referred to as the *connectome*.

There are now several recent initiatives that will enable better understanding of this complexity. These are large-scale, multicenter projects involving hundreds of scientists from all over the world, and from many research specialties: the Human Connectome Project (launched by National Institutes of Health in the United States, in 2010); the BRAIN (Brain Research through Advancing Innovative Neurotechnologies) Initiative, launched by President Obama in 2013; and the Human Brain Project (European Commission, 2013). There are amazing new research technologies that will advance this research. One example is *optogenetics*, which helps visualize living nerve cell activity inside animals; another is a process called *induced pluripotent stem cells* (where easily available cells—skin fibroblasts—can be converted to nerve cells, which then can be studied for uncovering disease markers). All of these projects and techniques will accelerate discoveries of biological bases of psychiatric disorders, and consequently will lead to the discovery of new treatments.

NEW IDEAS AND PROPOSALS ABOUT CLASSIFICATION OF PSYCHOTIC DISORDERS

Over a century ago, Dr. Emil Kraepelin made the distinction between affective (manic depressive) and non-affective psychotic disorders (dementia praecox, later called schizophrenia). This distinction continues into how we currently classify psychotic disorders, and persists in DSM-V (American Psychiatric Association, 2013) despite growing evidence for a considerable overlap between these two groups of disorders in terms of symptoms, outcome, treatment response, pathophysiology, and genetic causes.

Although the ICD and DSM have improved diagnostic *reliability* and have practical purposes, there are criticisms of the legitimacy of these diagnostic criteria. A major problem with *symptom-based* disorder categories is that they overlap a great deal in brain biology and risk factors. Psychiatric symptoms are better explained on *dimensional* rather than categorical lines. In other words, chopping up groups of psychiatric symptoms and trying to "fit" them into diagnostic categories is less useful than grouping symptoms on the basis of their biological mechanisms. Consequently, future refinements in diagnosis will probably come from advances in genetics and neurobiology.

Clinicians often notice that the clinical "picture" of individual patients may change over time. For example, someone diagnosed with a brief psychotic disorder initially may later meet diagnostic criteria of schizophreniform disorder or chronic schizophrenia, or may even recover and stay well. It is therefore argued that it makes little sense to use different diagnostic criteria when, in fact, they really reflect different manifestations of one underlying biological condition. Dr. Patrick McGorry (2006) has recently proposed a *staging* framework that may help clinicians think about changing manifestations of disease, that is, the prodromal phase (stage 1), schizophreniform disorders (stage 2), chronic, recurrent psychotic illness (stage 3), and chronic, persistent psychosis (stage 4). This approach, similar to that used in other medical diseases such as hypertension, offers an optimistic framework; thus, a patient may stay at, or recover from, stage 2, and not progress to stage 3 or 4 depending on treatment, and resilience. As our knowledge expands, it may be possible to define these stages based on brain-based biological markers.

Drs. Thomas Insel and Bruce Cuthbert from the National Institute of Mental Health have recently proposed an agnostic approach (meaning, without prejudging) to deriving research-based (diagnostic) entities by organizing what we scientifically know about a psychiatric disorder in order to advance research. Such *research domain criteria* (RDoC) may allow future researchers to classify psychotic disorders into neuroscience-based subtypes that may look quite different from current symptom-based categories. Such classifications (e.g., using a sequence of biomarkers) may be better in terms of predicting outcome and treatment response than current classification schemes (see Figure 18.1).

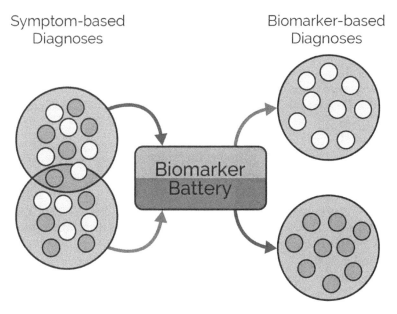

Symptom-based
Diagnoses

Biomarker-based
Diagnoses

Biomarker
Battery

Figure 18.1 Future Classifications of Psychoses Are Likely to Be Influenced by Underlying Biology

HOW TO DEVELOP BETTER TREATMENTS

The history of pharmacological treatments has largely been one of accidental discovery. The future, however, is likely to consist of developing drugs based on specific molecular characteristics. It is already possible to screen thousands of molecules to rapidly identify a handful that may have the possibility of becoming feasible treatments (high-throughput screening). Regardless of whether a drug is devised or discovered, there are many steps to be taken to determine safety, tolerability, and efficacy long before it can ever be released for public use. In the United States, the Federal Drug Administration (FDA) is responsible for ensuring that medicines that are approved for human use undergo rigorous testing.

Before a molecule in a laboratory ever becomes an approved treatment, there is a long scientific journey, which can take up to 15 years, and cost up to $1 billion. For every molecule that makes this journey successfully, as many as 10,000 compounds do not make the cut! It now may be understandable that new treatments for schizophrenia are not a regular occurrence.

Once a compound with clinical potential is identified, it undergoes thorough preclinical studies in the laboratory. After this, there are a series of increasingly rigorous human studies to determine safety and efficacy—is it safe and does it work? The following is a fairly standard progression of testing in human beings across the world:

- **Phase I** trial is conducted in a small group of people (20–80) to assess safety, dosage range, and possible side effects.
- **Phase II** trials are larger studies (100–300 subjects) to assess efficacy and safety.
- **Phase III** trials are large-scale studies (1,000–3,000 subjects), frequently multicountry, to confirm efficacy, compare with placebo or existing treatments, and ongoing monitoring of monitor.

Despite the enormous burden of developing new drugs, there are a number of promising compounds in the pipeline, many with novel mechanisms of action. According to PHRMA (www.phrma.org), there were 36 drugs under various stages of development for schizophrenia in 2014; some are listed in Table 18.1.

The high costs of and long delays in developing new drugs have recently, and unfortunately, led to a decline in pharmaceutical investments in this field. To address this, NIMH has been advocating the "experimental medicine" approach to accelerate drug discovery, which suggests that, in order for a clinical trial to proceed, the experimenter needs to (1) define a therapeutic target, (2) demonstrate target engagement, and (3) link the target engagement to the desired clinical outcome. Failure to do so at each stage will abort the trial, thus leading to a progressive increase in the number of likely "winners" that will move to the clinical trials phase.

Table 18.1 Small Selection of Drugs under Development

Compound	Mechanism of Action
NW-3509	Selectively blocks voltage-gated sodium channels (VGSCs)
IT-007	Serotonin 5-HT2A antagonist, a dopamine and glutamate phosphoprotein modulator, and a serotonin reuptake inhibitor
RP5063	Dopamine-serotonin system stabilizer
Encenicline	Nicotinic alpha-7-agonist
Cariprazine	Dopamine receptor partial agonists
Brexpiprazole	Dopamine receptor partial agonists

There is also an increasing emphasis on developing psychotherapeutic treatments, which have substantive effect sizes. Studies combining psychotherapy and drug treatments as well as brain stimulation approaches are also under way.

CAN WE PREVENT PSYCHOSES?

While prevention may be the ultimate goal of research efforts, is it even conceivable? Advances in understanding the *developmental origins* of psychotic disorders are now beginning to provide the push for *primary prevention* (preventing the illness for arising altogether) as a reasonable goal, particularly as we better understand the early risk factors and indicators of later emerging psychotic disorders. However, at the moment it is a theoretical concept, but one that researchers are thinking about actively.

Secondary Prevention

The notion of stopping a full-blown episode of psychosis from occurring is now within the realm of possibility. This idea is based on the observation that there are prodromal symptoms (subtle, psychotic-like symptoms) that may be caused by bursts of dopaminergic excess. Consequently, the use of low doses of APDs has been proposed. Because of the risk of significant side effects, such as weight gain, this approach needs to be used with caution. The notion of using APDs in all people who are at risk for developing schizophrenia, when in fact only about an unknown third of them might develop psychosis, presents significant ethical and practical dilemmas. Safer alternatives such as omega-3 fatty acids and cognitive behavior therapy have shown promise in preventing the onset of psychosis or decreasing the severity when it does develop.

SUMMARY

- Schizophrenia remains one of the grand challenges facing all of medicine.
- Small, incremental advances in our understanding of its nature and causes will go a long way to improving care, and personal and societal costs.
- While many unanswered questions remain, several promising new directions in research are under way, and are likely to significantly impact our approach to caring for people with schizophrenia.

Glossary

This is a list of some terms that you may have come across in this book, or terms that you may encounter when doing your own research (from trust-worthy sources) about schizophrenia. The list is by no means all-inclusive.

Some terms have multiple definitions, in which case the definition most relevant to schizophrenia is presented.

Acting-out Expressing emotional conflict or stress through behavior and actions without thinking or regard for (usually negative) consequences.

Affect Observable behavior that reflects the underlying emotion.

Affective blunting Sometimes called blunted affect. Significant reduction in the bodily, usually facial, expression of underlying emotions.

Agranulocytosis Granulocyte (a type of white blood cell) count below 500/ mm^3. This number becomes important primarily during treatment with clozapine.

Akathisia A feeling of physical restlessness (jitteriness) felt mostly in the legs, often accompanied by inability to sit still or lie quietly.

Allele One or more alternative forms of the same gene occupying the same place (locus) on a chromosome. Each person inherits two alleles for each gene, one from each parent.

Alogia Speech is brief, with simple responses, and little spontaneous speech; also called poverty of speech.

Anhedonia Inability to experience pleasure.

Anorgasmia Inability to achieve orgasm, even with adequate stimulation.

APD Abbreviation for antipsychotic drug.

Asociality Preferring to be alone and avoid social interaction.

Athetosis Slow, writhing movements, typically of the hands and feet; it is one of the movement types seen in TD.

Attention Attention is a mental process of *selectively concentrating* on one thing at a time while ignoring other stimuli. Compromised attention leads to distractibility.

Avolition   Lack of motivation in goal-directed activities.

Body mass index (BMI)   An indicator of extent of being overweight. There are two methods of calculating this number, depending on whether you use pounds or kilograms to measure weight. When using *pounds* (lbs.): weight in lbs. divided by height in inches, then multiplied by 703. When using *kilograms* (kg): weight in kg/square of height in meters. BMI between 25 and 30 is defined as overweight, 30 or more is considered obese.

Catatonia   Can present as either *catatonic stupor* (a general absence of motor activity) or *catatonic excitement* (violent, hyperactive behavior directed at oneself or others but with no visible purpose).

CATIE   Clinical Antipsychotic Trials of Intervention Effectiveness trial. Large-scale studies of the effectiveness of APDs from 2005/2006.

Chorea   Spontaneous irregular, abrupt, rapid movements involving limbs, face, and trunk, that can result in lurching "dance-like" gait.

Circumstantiality   Speech that is understandable, but has a lot irrelevant details that delay reaching the original point being made.

Cognition   A broad term referring to mental processes of knowing, including aspects such as awareness, reasoning, and judgment.

CT   Computed tomography or computerized axial tomography creates the image by using individual X-ray sensors that spin around the patient, permitting data from multiple angles. A computer processes this information to create an image.

CUtLASS   Cost Utility of the Latest Antipsychotic drugs in Schizophrenia Study; a large-scale study, published in 2006.

Cytochrome P450   A family of enzymes, primarily in the liver, responsible for breakdown of most drugs in the body. Of the 40–50 variations, there are two—2D6 and 3A4—that appear to be the most important for psychiatry.

Decompensation   Clinical worsening from current level of stability. This worsening can spontaneously return to previous level of stability without active treatment, or progress to a relapsed state.

Delirium   A reversible mental state that is recognized by confusion, disorientation, disordered thinking and memory, poor awareness, hyperactivity, and agitation. DSM V has specific diagnostic criteria.

Delusion   It is a fixed, false belief that is held in spite of evidence to the contrary, and is at out of context to the community's cultural and religious beliefs. It is also inconsistent with the level of education of the patient, and can be clearly absurd.

Dementia   Dementia is identified by loss of memory, confusion, understanding, and often with accompanying changes in personality and behavior. DSM V has specific diagnostic criteria.

Dendrites   Short, highly branched fibers that carry signals *toward* a nerve cell in the brain.

Denial   A psychological mechanism where unpleasant realities, whether internal or external, are kept out of awareness in order to avoid anxiety.

Derailment Also known as *loosening of associations*. Thinking that has very weak connections between one thought (usually a sentence) and the next. When it is severe, speech becomes completely incomprehensible.

Disorder Any deviation from the normal structure or function of any part, organ, or system of the body that is manifested by a characteristic set of symptoms and signs whose pathology and prognosis may be known or unknown (from Centers of Disease Control and Prevention).

Double-bind theory An outdated theory by Dr. Gregory Bateson (1956) about the origin of schizophrenia symptoms. This theory proposed repeated exposure to *conflicting messages* (usually, affection on the verbal level and hostility on the nonverbal level), without the opportunity to "escape" from them.

Double-blind design A type of treatment research design in which neither the participant nor the researcher knows what treatment the subject is receiving in order to minimize the likelihood of prejudicing the results of the study.

Downward drift hypothesis This theory basically states that the disability of schizophrenia leads toward lowered social and financial circumstances.

Dyskinesia Abnormal uncontrollable movements, such as tardive dyskinesia (TD).

Dysphoria A feeling of unpleasantness, unease, emotional discomfort.

Dystonia Muscle spasms, particularly of the tongue, jaw, eyes, and neck, and rarely of the whole body.

Echolalia Senseless repetition (echoing) of words or phrases that others say, right after it is said.

Echopraxia Senseless imitating or mirroring (echoing) the physical movements of others.

Effectiveness (of treatment) Whether a treatment works or not when used in real-life clinical conditions.

Efficacy Whether a treatment works under *experimental* conditions (not the same as effectiveness).

Emotion Appearance of naturally arising internal states of being, often associated by bodily changes. Basic emotions include anger, disgust, fear, joy, sadness, and surprise. However, there is little agreement over what comprises basic emotions.

Empathy Understanding what others are feeling because you have experienced it yourself or can put yourself "in their shoes." Not the same as sympathy, which is acknowledging another person's emotional hardships and providing comfort and assurance.

Empirical Knowledge that is based upon observation or experience, and capable of being tested by observation or experiment.

Endophenotype Also known as intermediate phenotype. A heritable trait or characteristic that is not actually a direct symptom of the condition but is *associated* with that condition.

EPS, Extrapyramidal symptoms Side effects of APDs that can resemble Parkinson's disease such as shakiness, stiffness, and slow movements. Restlessness and other involuntary movements may also be seen.

Erotomania A delusional belief that another person, usually of a higher social status, is in love with them.

Ethnicity The classification of a population that shares a common culture and national origin.

Executive functions Higher-level psychological functions involved in setting goals, planning, self-regulating, and completing an intended task.

Expressed emotion Negative communication by family members involving excessive criticism, emotional over-involvement, and intrusiveness directed at a patient.

Faith The personal aspects of religion. Among its many meanings are loyalty to a religion or religious community or its tenets, commitment to a relationship with God and belief in the existence of God.

Flat affect Absent or almost absent in affective (emotional) expression.

Flight of ideas Speech that is recognized by abrupt changes from topic to topic, but with a generally *understandable connection* between topics.

fMRI Functional MRI used to measure blood flow changes related to brain activity; the amount of blood flow is believed to reflect the amount of underlying brain activity.

Gender One's own sense of being masculine or feminine, which is largely determined by culture. This is not the same as biological sex.

Gene A unit of hereditary transmission of a trait within families.

Gliosis Increase of glia (a type of brain cell) in damaged areas of the central nervous system ("scarring").

Grandiose Overestimating oneself (worth, power, importance, knowledge, position); it can become a grandiose delusion when severe and persistent. It is seen in mania and schizophrenia.

Gustatory Pertaining to the sense of taste.

Hallucination False sensation *without* any external trigger, and can affect hearing, vision, taste, smell, and touch.

Heritability It is a complex notion, which basically tries to estimate how much genetics contributes to a characteristic or trait in a person. With schizophrenia, there is high heritability; in other words, genes play a major role.

Hyperprolactinemia Increased levels of prolactin in the blood (a hormone associated with milk production in women). It is associated with problems with the menstrual period.

Hypochondriacal False belief that one is suffering from a serious illness.

Ideas of reference Incorrect interpretations of harmless incidents, or that belief that external events have personal meaning.

Illusion False sensation *with* an external trigger, and can affect hearing, vision, taste, smell, and touch.

Inappropriate affect Emotional responses that appear not to match the situation or thinking at the time.

Incidence Number of newly diagnosed cases during a specific time period.

Insight Awareness and understanding. In the case of schizophrenia, some patients are unaware (lack insight) that they have this illness.

Labile, lability   Abnormal changeability in emotional expression, with abrupt and unpredictable shifts in mood.

Leukopenia   Decrease in total number of leukocytes (white blood cells).

Lifetime prevalence   The number of individuals in the population who will develop the disorder *at some point* during their lifetime.

Lobotomy   It is a completely outmoded surgical interruption of nerve connections to and from the frontal lobe of the brain, first introduced in 1936 by the neurologist Dr. Egas Moniz. The goal was to treat stubborn cases of schizophrenia.

Loose associations   Thinking that has very weak connections between one thought (usually a sentence) and the next. When it is severe, speech becomes completely incomprehensible. Also known as *derailment*.

LSD   Lysergic acid diethylamide, a hallucinogenic drug that can result in schizophrenia-like symptoms.

Magical thinking   Belief that one's thoughts, words, or actions can result in an action that defies normal laws of cause and effect; in other words it is an impossible idea.

Mannerisms   Purposeful actions carried out in an odd or unnatural fashion.

MRI   Magnetic resonance imaging is a technique that uses a magnetic field and radio waves to create detailed images of the organs, including, within the body.

Multifactorial   When the presentation of an illness is determined by multiple genetic and nongenetic factors.

Negative symptoms   A cluster of symptoms recognized by decrease of mental function that is frequently accompanied by bodily symptoms (alogia, affective flattening, anhedonia, asociality, avolition and apathy, and attentional impairment).

Neologism   Invention of new word or the highly personal use of a standard word ("my arm was fenestrated" [meaning fractured]).

Neuroleptic   Another name for an antipsychotic drug, that was named in 1952 by Dr. Delay; he also introduced chlorpromazine, the first APD, to psychiatry.

Neuropil   Brain tissue that lies between the nerve cells.

Neutropenia   Decreased amount of neutrophils (a type of white blood cell).

Olfaction   The sense of smell.

Orthostatic hypotension   Drop in blood pressure, generally after getting up or standing up too quickly, leading to lightheadedness and dizziness, which may cause falls.

Overvalued idea   An *unreasonable* belief that is held less strongly than a delusion. This thinking has to be out of line with the community's cultural and religious beliefs.

Paranoia   Irrational fear, suspicion, or distrust of others, which may become a paranoid delusion.

Paraphrenia   An outdated term that refers to late-onset schizophrenia (after the age of 45 years).

Parkinsonism   Having the characteristics of Parkinson's disease (tremor, rigidity, slowed body movements, instability, and shuffling gait).

PCP Phencyclidine, a hallucinogenic drug that can result in schizophrenia-like symptoms.

Perception The process of acquiring, interpreting, and organizing sensory information from the environment or one's own body.

Perinatal A term for the time period between when the fetus (unborn baby) is 20 weeks old up to 28 days after birth.

Perseveration The *inappropriate and excessive* repeating of speech or physical actions that were appropriate during the *previous* task.

PET Positron emission tomography is method for imaging brain blood flow (assumed to reflect brain activity) by using radioactive tracers that are injected into the bloodstream.

Point prevalence The number of individuals within a population affected by a particular disease at a *single* point in time (e.g., a year) divided by the total number of people in that population.

Polygenic Expression of a disorder caused by the interaction of multiple genes, each of which has a relatively small overall effect.

Polymorphism Variation in the structure of the gene (DNA sequences) among 1–2% of the population, permitting genetic studies.

PORT Schizophrenia Patient Outcome Research Team; expert panel treatment recommendations published in 2010.

Positive symptoms The symptoms seen in schizophrenia (delusions, hallucinations, thought disorder).

Posturing The assumption of odd postures.

Poverty of content of speech Speech is adequate or even excessive in *amount* but conveys very little information because it contains unnecessary details, and is vague, overly literal, and repetitive.

Poverty of speech Speech is recognized by very brief and simple responses, and little spontaneous speech; also called *alogia*.

Prefrontal cortex Part of the brain (gray matter) in the front portion of the brain, right behind the forehead. It is highly developed in humans and plays an important role complex thinking, emotions, and behavior.

Premorbid Before the onset of an illness.

Prevalence Frequency of new and old (living) cases within a population at given time point.

Prognosis A forecast of the probable course of disease.

Psychoeducation It is education (for patient and family) to improve overall treatment and rehabilitation; it includes information about the illness and its treatment, identifying signs of relapse, coping strategies and problem-solving skills.

Psychosis Psychosis is a state identified by losing touch with reality, and includes false beliefs (delusions), false perceptions (hallucinations), irrational thinking, and behaviors.

QTc interval It is a measure of the way the heart is beating, assessed by examining the EKG. When interval (time period) is increased, there is risk of heart problems. Some medications, including APDs, can increase the QTc interval.

Race Distinct human groups commonly identified on the basis of skin color, facial features, ancestry, genetics, or national origin.

Recovery The absence of symptoms and return to premorbid level of functioning.

Relapse It is generally understood to mean clinical worsening that requires active intervention (adjustment of antipsychotic dose, even hospitalization).

Restricted affect Noticeable reduction in emotional expression, but not as severe as blunted affect.

Self-efficacy A term refers to the ability to cope with a situation, or a sense of our capacities; it is a concept that is important in the self-management of schizophrenia.

Sialorrhea Drooling or excessive salivation.

Single-blind design A type of (clinical) experiment in which the participant does not know which treatment he or she is receiving, in order to minimize the expectations of a specific effect.

Somatic Awareness of a physical experience localized within the body.

Somatosensory Perception originating elsewhere in the body other than in the special sense organs (e.g., eyes).

Stereotypies Non-purposeful and uniformly repetitive motions, such as tapping and rocking.

Stigma Being labeled on the basis of an illness or condition. Being put into stereotyped groups. Negative attitudes lead to prejudice, negative actions and discrimination.

Stupor A mental state characterized by extreme inactivity and lack of response without a loss of consciousness.

Syndrome Group or recognizable pattern of signs and symptoms or phenomena that indicate a particular trait or disease; the presence of one feature of the group alerts to the presence of the others.

Tangentiality A form of thought disturbance in which thoughts/speech starts off in the correct direction but quickly strays to unrelated areas without ever returning to the original point.

Tardive dyskinesia Late (*tardive*) onset abnormal movements characterized by non-rhythmic choreiform (jerky) or athetoid (slow writhing) movements typically affecting the tongue, lips, jaw, fingers, toes, and trunk. TD can be transient or permanent.

THC Tetrahydrocannabinol—the chemical compound in marijuana responsible for its brain effects.

Therapeutic alliance Collaborative relationship between patient and therapist.

Thought blocking In mid-sentence the patient appears to have lost the train of thought.

Thought broadcasting A delusional belief that others can sense, and even read, your thoughts.

Thought insertion Belief or experience that outside forces place thoughts into one's mind.

Titration Stepwise increase or decrease in the dose of a medication.

Word salad Unconnected words or short meaningless phrases that make the speech totally incomprehensible.

SECTION 6

Appendices

APPENDIX A

Commonly Used Antipsychotics for Schizophrenia

*C*aveat (from Latin, "let him beware"): Use the following table *only* as a guide, not for adjusting the dose on your own!

ANTIPSYCHOTIC DRUGS

	Name	Usual Daily Dose, mg	Common Side Effects
Second-Generation APDs	Aripiprazole	10–30	Headache, anxiety, insomnia, nausea and vomiting, dizziness, akathisia, sedation
	Asenapine	5–20	Sedation, tingling around mouth, orthostatic hypotension, upset stomach
	Clozapine	100–600	Sedation, orthostatic hypotension, excessive salivation, anticholinergic effects, weight gain, dyslipidemias, hyperthermia, tachycardia, seizures, agranulocytosis, new-onset DM
	Iloperidone	2–24	Sedation, orthostatic hypotension, dry mouth, stuffy nose
	Lurasidone	40–160	Sedation, anxiety, restlessness
	Olanzapine	5–20	Sedation, orthostatic hypotension, weight gain, dyslipidemias, new-onset DM
	Quetiapine	150–900	Sedation, orthostatic hypotension, transient weight gain, dyslipidemias, new-onset DM
	Risperidone	2–6	EPS, increased prolactin, sedation, orthostatic hypotension, weight gain, dyslipidemias, new-onset DM
	Ziprasidone	40–160	Q-Tc prolongation, sedation, orthostatic hypotension, new-onset DM

(*Continued*)

	Name	Usual Daily Dose, mg	Common Side Effects
First-Generation APDs	Chlorpromazine	150–1000	Sedation, orthostatic hypotension, EPS, photosensitivity, jaundice, TD, seizures, agranulocytosis, anticholinergic effects, weight gain
	Fluphenazine	2–20	EPS, TD, weight gain
	Haloperidol	2–25	EPS, TD, weight gain
	Loxapine	30–150	Sedation, orthostatic hypotension, EPS, TD, seizures, anticholinergic effects, weight gain
	Perphenazine	16–64	Sedation, orthostatic hypotension, EPS, TD, seizures, anticholinergic effects, weight gain
	Pimozide	2–12	EPS, TD, weight gain
	Thiothixene	6–50	EPS, TD, weight gain
	Trifluoperazine	5–30	Sedation, orthostatic hypotension, EPS, TD, seizures, anticholinergic effects, weight gain

EPS: extrapyramidal symptoms; DM: diabetes mellitus

APPENDIX B

Very Brief History of Schizophrenia

Schizophrenia has not always been known as *schizophrenia*!

Schizophrenia, *as a name*, is a little over a hundred years old. Some psychiatric historians suggest that schizophrenia (as a clinical condition) is an ancient disorder, while others argue that it is a relatively modern one, not more than two centuries old. There exist very early writings, as far back 2,000–3,000 years ago, from Egypt, Mesopotamia, and India, which contain descriptions of mental disorder. However, most historians agree that descriptions similar to the current notions of schizophrenia show up only in the 18th century.

The history of schizophrenia is really a history of excellent *clinical observation*, by clinicians who learned to *understand* their patients and care for them over long periods of time, even entire lifetimes. This provided the opportunity to detect *patterns* of symptoms and outcomes among a variety of illnesses, allowing separation into different clinical syndromes. This was occurring primarily during the 19th century when there was a great deal of interest in disease classification (nosology), leading to a number of different systems to categorize mental disorders.

Some of the important contributors to today's and future concepts of schizophrenia are listed in the following table. Before the availability of imaging techniques (CT, MRI) it was not possible to identify brains areas that may be important on schizophrenia; these contributions were "practical" but of vital importance for advancing our understanding of schizophrenia. These scientific advances will change our ideas about schizophrenia, and one day, this condition may no longer be referred to as schizophrenia!

IMPORTANT CONTRIBUTIONS TO THE CONCEPT AND RESEARCH DIRECTIONS IN SCHIZOPHRENIA

Name	Date of Contribution	Contributions
Phillipe Pinel	1790s	He invented *moral treatment*
Jean-Étienne Dominique Esquirol	1810	Monomania
Charles Lasègue	1852	Delusion of persecution
Benedict Morel	1860	He introduced the term *dementia praecoce*
Ewald Hecker	1871	He gave us *hebephrenia*
Karl Kahlbaum	1874	He coined the term "catatonia" (*katatonia*)
Emil Kraepelin	1899	He presented the distinction between *dementia praecox* and manic-depressive psychosis
Eugen Bleuler	1908	He coined the term *schizophrenia* Bleuler's *four As* (autism, ambivalence, disturbances in association, and affectivity)
Sigmund Freud	1911	He introduced concepts of *projection* and primary *narcissism*
Adolf Meyer	1920s–1950s	He considered schizophrenia was caused by harmful habits in conjunction with biological factors as well as heredity
Gabriel Langfeldt	1939	He identified *schizophreniform* states
American Psychiatric Association	1952	First edition of the *Diagnostic and Statistical Manual of Mental Disorders* (DSM)—schizophrenia is considered an organic brain disorder
Kurt Schneider	1959	He defined the *first rank symptoms*
David Ingvar and Goran Franzen	1974	He developed a method to measure decreased blood flow to the frontal lobes, prompting attention to this brain area
Eve Johnstone and colleagues	1976	First CT study in schizophrenia, finding enlarged brain ventricles
American Psychiatric Association	1980	Third edition of DSM; schizophrenia diagnosis focuses on deterioration aspect of the diagnosis

Daniel Weinberger	1986	The *DLPFC hypothesis* (dorsolateral prefrontal cortex area of the brain) explaining both positive and negative symptoms
Dilip Jeste	1997	He proposed the concept of *late-onset schizophrenia*
Patrick McGorry	2006	*Staging framework* for schizophrenia and related disorders.
Thomas Insel and Bruce Cuthbert	2010	The Research Diagnostic Criteria (R-DoC) was proposed as a way to organize what we know across translational domains
American Psychiatric Association	2013	Fifth edition of DSM; subtyping categories of schizophrenia removed, and "first rank" symptoms no longer separately important
Schizophrenia Working Group	2014	108 genetic loci were discovered as underlying schizophrenia in the largest genome-wide study to date of schizophrenia

APPENDIX C

Recommended Resources

Looking for further information on navigating a schizophrenia diagnosis? Any of the following resources will help provide answers to the questions you have about living with schizophrenia. Those sources that the authors like or use are **bolded**.

ESSENTIAL READING

Amador, Xavier. *I Am Not Sick, I Don't Need Help!* 10th Anniversary Edition. Peconic, NY: Vida Press, 2010 (ISBN: 0967718953).

Karp, David. *Burden of Sympathy: How Families Cope with Mental Illness.* New York: Oxford University Press, 2000 (ISBN: 0195152441).

Levine, Jerome, and Irene Levine. *Schizophrenia for Dummies.* New York: Wiley, 2009 (ISBN: 0470259272).

Marsh, Diane T., and Rex Dickens. *How to Cope with Mental Illness in Your Family: A Self-Care Guide for Siblings, Offspring, and Parents.* New York: Putnam, 1997 (ISBN: 0874779235).

Russell, L. Mark, and Arnold E. Grant. *Planning for the Future: Providing a Meaningful Life for a Child with a Disability after Your Death, 5th Edition.* Palatine, IL: Planning for the Future Inc., 2005 (ISBN: 0912891203).

Torrey, E Fuller. *Surviving Schizophrenia: A Manual for Families, Consumers, and Providers, 6th Edition.* New York: Harper Collins Publications, 2013 (ISBN: 0062268856).

Woolis, Rebecca. *When Someone You Love Has a Mental Illness: A Handbook for Family, Friends and Caregivers.* New York: Perigee Books, 1992 (ISBN: 0874776953).

Wright, Nicola, Douglas Turkington, Owen Kelly, David Davies, Andrew Jacobs, and Jennifer Hopton. *Treating Psychosis.* Oakland, CA: New Harbinger Publications Inc., 2014 (ISBN: 1608824071).

GENERAL READING AND BOOKS ON THE EXPERIENCE OF SCHIZOPHRENIA

Andreasen, Nancy. *Brave New Brain: Conquering Mental Illness in the Era of the Genome.* New York: Oxford University Press, 2004 (ISBN: 0195167287).

Deveson, Anne. *Tell Me I'm Here.* New York: Penguin Books, 1992 (ISBN: 0140173390).

Earley, Pete. *Crazy: A Father's Search through America's Mental Health Madness.* New York: G.P. Putnam's Sons, 2006 (ISBN: 0399153136).

Holley, Tara E., and Joe Holley. *My Mother's Keeper: A Daughter's Memoir of Growing Up in the Shadow of Schizophrenia.* New York: Morrow, 1997 (ISBN: 0380723026).

Inman, Susan. *After Her Brain Broke: Helping My Daughter Recover Her Sanity.* Dundas, Ontario: Bridgeross Communications, 2010 (ISBN: 0981003788).

Jamison, Kay R. *An Unquiet Mind: A Memoir of Moods and Madness.* New York: Knopf, 1995 (ISBN: 0679443746).

Kaye, Randy. *Ben Behind His Voices: One Family's Journey from the Chaos of Schizophrenia to Hope.* Lanham, MD: Rowman & Littlefield Publishers, 2011 (ISBN: 1442210893).

McLean, Richard. *Recovered, Not Cured: A Journey through Schizophrenia.* Crows Nest, Australia: Allen and Unwin, 2005 (ISBN: 1865089745).

Moorman, Margaret. *My Sister's Keeper.* New York: Norton, 1992 (ISBN: 0393324044).

Nasar, Sylvia. *A Beautiful Mind.* New York: Simon and Schuster, 2011 (ISBN: 1451628420).

Saks, Elyn R. *The Center Cannot Hold.* New York: Hyperion, 2007 (ISBN: 140130138X).

Sheehan, Susan. *Is There No Place on Earth for Me?* New York: Vintage Books, 2014 (ISBN: 0804169187).

Simon, Clea. *Mad House: Growing Up in the Shadow of Mentally Ill Siblings.* New York: Doubleday, 1997 (ISBN: 0385478526).

Winerip, Michael. *9 Highland Road.* New York: Pantheon Books, 1994 (ISBN: 0679407243).

Wyden, Peter. *Conquering Schizophrenia: A Father, His Son, and a Medical Breakthrough.* New York: Knopf, 1998 (ISBN: 0679446710).

Yeiser, Bethany. *Mind Estranged: My Journey from Schizophrenia and Homelessness to Recovery.* Bethany Yeiser, 2014 (ISBN: 099034522X).

WEBSITES

The Internet has been a tremendous boon to both patients and practitioners alike. With increasing worldwide access to websites, patients and their loved ones can benefit by sharing their personal experiences in a way that was unimaginable only a few years ago. The following resources are great places to find additional, up-to-date information.

General Websites

American Academy of Adolescent and Child Psychology—www.aacap.org
American Psychiatric Association—www.psych.org
Brain & Behavior Research Foundation—www.bbrfoundation.org
Choices in Recovery—www.choicesinrecovery.com
Internet Mental Health—www.mentalhealth.com
Medscape—www.medscape.com
Mental Health America—www.mentalhealthamerica.net
National Alliance on Mental Illness—www.nami.org
National Association of State Mental Health Programs—www.nasmhpd.org
National Federation of Families for Children's Mental Health—www.ffcmh.org
Psych Central—www.psychcentral.com
Psych Guides—www.psychguides.com
ReThink—www.rethink.org
Schizophrenia 24x7—www.schizophrenia24x7.com
Schizophrenia and Related Disorders Alliance of America—www.sardaa.org
Schizophrenia.com—www.schizophrenia.com
Schizophrenic.com—www.schizophrenic.com
Time to Change—www.time-to-change.org.uk

Government Agencies

Centers for Medicare and Medicaid Services—www.cms.hhs.gov
Homelessness Resource Center—homeless.samhsa.gov
National Health Information Center—www.healthfinder.gov
National Institute of Mental Health—www.nimh.nih.gov
National Institute on Alcohol Abuse and Alcoholism—www.niaaa.nih.gov
National Institute on Drug Abuse—www.drugabuse.gov
National Institutes of Health—www.health.nih.gov
National Mental Health Information Center—www.mentalhealth.gov
Pubmed—www.ncbi.nlm.nih.gov/pubmed
Social Security Administration—www.ssa.gov
Substance Abuse and Mental Health Services Administration—www.samhsa.gov
U.S. Department of Housing and Urban Development—www.hud.gov
U.S. Department of Veterans Affairs Mental Health—www.mentalhealth.va.gov
U.S. Government Clinical Trials—www.clinicaltrials.gov

Medical Resources

Benefits Checkup—www.benefitscheckup.org
Benefit Finder—www.benefits.gov/benefits/benefit-finder

FDA Drug Database—www.fda.gov/Drugs/default.htm
Healthcare.gov—www.healthcare.gov
Needy Meds—www.needymeds.org
Partnership for Prescription Assistance—www.pparx.org
Patient Advocate Foundation—www.patientadvocate.org
Patient Advocate Foundation Copay Relief—www.copays.org

Caregiver Support

Caregiver Action Network—www.nfcacares.org
Caregiver Resource Network—www.caregiverresource.net
The Caregiver Space—www.thecaregiverspace.org
CaringBridge—www.caringbridge.org
Caring.com—www.caring.com
Caring Wise—www.caringwise.com
Don't Lose Heart—www.dontloseheart.org
National Alliance for Caregiving—www.caregiving.org
Personal Health Records—www.myphr.com
Share the Care—www.sharethecare.org

Schizophrenia and Mental Health Blogs

Brain Blogger—www.brainblogger.com
The Mental Elf—www.thementalelf.net
Pete Earley—www.peteearley.com
The Schizophrenic Writer—www.schizophrenicwriter.com
Serious Mental Illness Blog—www.seriousmentalillness.net
Suicidal No More—www.suicidalnomore.com

EARLY PSYCHOSIS TREATMENT AND RESEARCH CENTERS

The following are a few centers that are known for pioneering work on early psychosis. If you are interested in learning more, contact each center directly for more information on research and clinical services:

CAPPS (Center for the Assessment and Prevention of Prodromal States)

Depts. Of Psychology and Psychiatry & Biobehavioral Sciences
UCLA
Neuropsychiatric Institute
300 Building Medical Plaza
Los Angeles, CA 90095
Tel: (310) 206–3466

CARE (Cognitive Assessment and Risk Evaluation) Program

University of San Diego, California (UCSD) Outpatient Psychiatry Clinic
140 Arbor Drive
San Diego, CA 92103
Tel: (619) 543–7795

COPE (The Center of Prevention & Evaluation)

Department of Psychiatry/New York State Psychiatric Institute
Columbia University
4th Floor, Room 4820
1051 Riverside Drive
New York, NY 10032
Tel: (212) 543–5874

Developmental Processes in the Early Course of Illness

Dept. of Psychiatry and Biobehavioral Sciences
UCLA
405 Hilgard Ave.
Los Angeles, CA 90095
Tel: (310) 825–0036

EAST (Early Assessment and Support Team)

Mid-Valley Behavioral Care Network
1660 Oak Street SE, #230
Salem, OR 97301
Tel: (888) 315–6822

EDAPT (Early Diagnosis and Preventive Treatment)

2230 Stockton Boulevard
Sacramento, CA 95817
Tel: (916) 734–2964

FEPP (First Episode and Early Psychosis Program)

Department of Psychiatry Wang Building, Suite 805
Massachusetts General Hospital
55 Fruit Street
Boston, MA 02114
Tel: (617) 912–7800

First Episode Clinic

Maryland Psychiatric Research Center
University of Maryland School of Medicine

Tawes Ct
Catonsville, MD 21228
Tel: (410) 402–6833

First Episode Program
University of Illinois Hospital
912 S. Wood Street
Chicago, IL 60612
Tel: (312) 996–7383

PART (Prodrome Assessment Research and Treatment) Program
The Langley Porter Psychiatric Institute
University of California, San Francisco (UCSF)
401 Parnassus Avenue
San Francisco, CA 94143
Tel: (415) 476–7278

PIER (Portland Identification and Early Referral) Program
Maine Medical Center
315 Park Avenue
Portland, ME 04102
Tel: (207) 662–2004

PREP (Prevention and Recovery in Early Psychosis)
Massachusetts Mental Health Center
180 Morton Street
Jamaica Plain, MA 02130
Tel: (617) 626–9300

PRIME (Prevention through Risk Identification Management and Education)
Yale Psychiatric Institute
Yale University
184 Liberty Street
PO Box 208038
New Haven, CT 06520
Tel: (203) 785–7210

RAPP (Recognition and Prevention of Psychological Problems)
Psychiatry Research
Hillside Hospital

75–59 263 Street
Glen Oaks, NY 11004
Tel: (718) 470–8034

STEP (Services for the Treatment of Early Psychosis)

Western Psychiatric Institute and Clinic
3811 O'Hara Street
Pittsburgh, PA 15213
Tel: (412) 586–9009

ANTIPSYCHOTIC DRUG MANUFACTURERS

The following table includes primary telephone numbers and website addresses for antipsychotic drug manufacturers, who may be able to put you in touch with prescription assistance.

Drug	Manufacturer	Toll-free Number	Company Website
Aripiprazole (Abilify)	Bristol-Myers Squibb Co.	(800) 736–0003	www.bms.com
Asenapine (Saphris)	Forest Pharmaceuticals	(800) 678–1605	www.frx.com
Chlorpromazine (Thorazine, Largactil)	GlaxoSmithKline	(888) 825–5249	www.gsk.com
Clozapine (Clozaril)	Novartis Pharmaceuticals	(888) 669–6682	www.novartis.com
Flupenthixol (Fluanxol, Depixol)	Lundbeck	(866) 337–6996	www.lundbeck.com
Fluphenazine (Prolixn, Permitil)	Bristol-Myers Squibb Co.	(800) 736–0003	www.bms.com
Haloperidol (Haldol)	Janssen Pharmaceuticals	(800) 526–7736	www.janssen.com
Iloperidone (Fanapt)	Novartis Pharmaceuticals	(888) 669–6682	www.novartis.com
Loxapine (Loxitane)	Actavis Pharmaceuticals	(862) 261–7000	www.actavis.com
Lurasidone (Latuda)	Sunovion Pharmaceuticals	(855) 552–8832	www.sunovion.com
Olanzapine (Zyprexa, Zydis)	Eli Lilly & Co.	(800) 545–5979	www.lilly.com
Paliperidone (Invega)	Janssen Pharmaceuticals	(800) 526–7736	www.janssen.com
Perphenazine (Trilafon)	Bayer Pharmaceuticals	(888) 842–2937	www.pharma.bayer.com
Pimozide (Orap)	Gate Pharmaceuticals	(800) 292–4283	www.gatepharma.com
Quetiapine (Seroquel)	AstraZeneca Pharmaceuticals	(800) 292–6363	www.astrazeneca-us.com
Risperidone (Risperidal, Consta)	Janssen Pharmaceuticals	(800) 526–7736	www.janssen.com
Thioridazine (Mellaril)	Novartis Pharmaceuticals	(888) 669–6682	www.novartis.com
Thiothixene (Navane)	Pfizer Inc.	(800) 879–3477	www.pfizer.com
Trifluoperazine (Stelazine)	GlaxoSmithKline	(888) 825–5249	www.gsk.com
Ziprasidone (Geodon)	Pfizer Inc.	(800) 879–3477	www.pfizer.com
Zotepine (Zoleptil)	Orion Pharma	(358) 10–4261	www.orion.fi

APPENDIX D

Forms and Lists

FORMS:

ID AND EMERGENCY CONTACT INFO
MEDICATIONS
HOSPITALIZATIONS

LISTS:

EARLY SIGNS SCALE
ABCDs of STRENGTHS INVENTORY
COMMON FOODS—HEALTHY and UNHEALTHY

USE THESE FORMS AS THEY ARE OR ADAPT THEM TO YOUR NEEDS.

MAKE COPIES.

USE THEM!

ID AND EMERGENCY INFO
PRINT IN BLOCK LETTERS

NAME:	Date of Birth:	SSN:	MRN:
Tel No:	ADDRESS:		

EMERGENCY CONTACT

NAME:	Tel No:	Email:
ADDRESS:		

EMERGENCY CONTACT

NAME:	Tel No:	Email:
ADDRESS:		

MEDICAL CONTACT (PSYCHIATRIST)

NAME:	Tel No:	Email:
ADDRESS:		

MEDICAL CONTACT (PRIMARY CARE PHYSICIAN)

NAME:	Tel No:	Email:
ADDRESS:		

MEDICATIONS
PRINT IN BLOCK LETTERS

NAME: Date of Birth: MRN:

ALLERGIES:

Name and Dose	Date Started	Date Stopped	Side Effects/Reason Medicine Stopped

HOSPITALIZATIONS
PRINT IN BLOCK LETTERS

NAME: Date of Birth: MRN:

ALLERGIES:

Date Hospitalized	Date Discharged	Hospital Name	Reason for Hospitali- zation	Treatment If Known	Doctors Names

EARLY SIGNS SCALE (ESS)

Thinking and Perception	Feelings	Behaviors
Thoughts are racing	Feeling helpless or useless	Difficulty sleeping
Senses seem sharper	Feeling afraid of going crazy	Speech comes out jumbled filled with odd words
Thinking you have special powers	Feeling sad or low	Talking or smiling to yourself
Thinking that you can read other people's minds	Feeling anxious and restless	Acting suspiciously as if being watched
Thinking that other people can read your mind	Feeling increasingly religious	Behaving oddly for no reason
Receiving personal messages from the TV or radio	Feeling like you're being watched	Spending time alone
Having difficulty making decisions	Feeling isolated	Neglecting your appearance
Experiencing strange sensations	Feeling tired or lacking energy	Acting like you are somebody else
Preoccupied about 1 or 2 things	Feeling confused or puzzled	Not seeing people
Thinking you might be somebody else	Feeling forgetful or far away	Not eating
Seeing visions or things others cannot see	Feeling in another world	Not leaving the house
Thinking people are talking about you	Feeling strong and powerful	Behaving like a child
Thinking people are against you	Feeling unable to cope with everyday tasks	Refusing to do simple requests
Having more nightmare	Feeling like you are being punished	Drinking more
Having difficulty concentrating	Feeling like you cannot trust other people	Smoking more
Thinking bizarre things	Feeling irritable	Movements are slow
Thinking your thoughts are controlled	Feeling like you do not need sleep	Unable to sit down for long
Hearing voices	Feeling guilty	Behaving aggressively
Thinking that a part of you has changed shape		

Source: Birchwood M, et al. (1989): Predicting relapse in schizophrenia: the development and implementation of an early signs monitoring system using patients and families as observers, a preliminary investigation. *Psychol Med* 19:649–56

ABCDs OF STRENGTHS INVENTORY

	Is This Your Strength?	Is This a Strength You Wish to Develop?
ADHERENCE Do you take medicines as prescribed? Do you adhere to regular appointments with your care team?		
BEDTIMES Do you go to bed and wake up at regular times? Do you sleep well?		
COMMUNITY Are you involved in community activities?		
DRUGS AND ALCOHOL Do you stay away from street drugs, smoking and alcohol?		
EXERCISE Do you like to exercise and be physically fit?		
FOOD Do you eat regularly? Do you eat healthy foods		
GOALS Do you set clear goals for recovery?		
HELP Are you involved in self-help/ advocacy/ peer support groups?		
INFORMATION Are you well informed about health and mental health issues?		
JOYOUS ACTIVITIES Do you enjoy recreational activities (such as art, music, movies, TV)?		

COMMON FOODS—HEALTHY AND UNHEALTHY
(ALPHABETICAL)

Healthy	Unhealthy
Apples	Soda
Bananas	Fried chicken
Beans (all kinds)	Egg and sausage sandwich
Broccoli	Bacon cheeseburger
Brown rice	French fries
Canned salmon	Milkshake
Canned tomatoes	Deep fried cheese sticks
Canned tuna	Mayonnaise
Cantaloupe	Pepperoni pizza
Carrots	Nachos
Chicken breasts	Hot dogs
Cottage cheese	Chicken nuggets
Eggs	Ice cream
Garbanzo beans	Creamy salad dressing
Kale	Processed luncheon salads
Lentils	Sugared cereal
Low-fat milk	Cheeseburger
Oats	Candy bars
Olive oil	Chips
Onions	White bread
Oranges	Cookies
Peanuts (not peanut butter)	Sugared drinks
Pears	Apple juice
Popcorn (without butter)	Grape juice
Pumpkin seeds	Margarine
Spinach	
Sweet potatoes	
Tofu	
Watermelon	
Whole wheat bread	
Whole-grain pasta	
Yogurt	

REFERENCES

American Psychiatric Association (2013): *Diagnostic and Statistical Manual of Mental Disorders* (5th ed.; DSM–5), American Psychiatric Publishing Arlington, VA.

Andreasen NC (1989): The Scale for the Assessment of Negative Symptoms (SANS): conceptual and theoretical foundations. *Br J Psychiatry Suppl*:49–58.

Andreasen NC, Carpenter WT, Jr., Kane JM, Lasser RA, Marder SR, Weinberger DR (2005): Remission in schizophrenia: proposed criteria and rationale for consensus. *Am J Psychiatry* 162:441–49.

Birchwood M, Smith J, Macmillan F, et al. (1989): Predicting relapse in schizophrenia: the development and implementation of an early signs monitoring system using patients and families as observers, a preliminary investigation. *Psychol Med* 19:649–56.

Braham LG, Trower P, Birchwood M (2004): Acting on command hallucinations and dangerous behavior: a critique of the major findings in the last decade. *Clin Psychol Rev* 4:513–28.

Citrome L (2013): New second-generation long-acting injectable antipsychotics for the treatment of schizophrenia. *Expert Rev Neurother* 13(7): 767–83.

Clement S et al. (2013): Mass media interventions for reducing mental health-related stigma. *Cochrane Database Syst Rev* 23(7):CD009453.

Collins PY et al. (2011): Grand challenges in global mental health. *Nature* 475(7354): 27–30.

Cross-Disorder Group of the Psychiatric Genomics Consortium (2013): Identification of risk loci with shared effects on five major psychiatric disorders: a genome-wide analysis. *Lancet* 20;381(9875): 1371–79.

Dold M, Leucht S (2014): Pharmacotherapy of treatment-resistant schizophrenia: a clinical perspective. *Evid Based Ment Health* 17(2): 33–37.

Duckworth K, Halpern L (May 2014): Peer support and peer-led family support for persons living with schizophrenia. *Curr Opin Psychiatry* 27(3): 216–21.

Gottesman II, Gould TD (2003): The endophenotype concept in psychiatry: etymology and strategic intentions. *Am J Psychiatry* 160(4): 636–45.

Gratten J et al. (2014): Large-scale genomics unveils the genetic architecture of psychiatric disorders. *Nat Neurosci* 17(6): 782–90.

Harvey PD (2014): What is the evidence for changes in cognition and functioning over the lifespan in patients with schizophrenia? *J Clin Psychiatry* 75 (Suppl 2): 34–38.

Henderson AR (2013): The impact of social cognition training on recovery from psychosis. *Curr Opin Psychiatry* 26(5): 429–32.

Hogarty GE, Flesher S, Ulrich R et al. (2004): Cognitive enhancement therapy for schizophrenia: effects of a 2-year randomized trial on cognition and behavior. *Arch Gen Psychiatry* 61: 866–76.

Insel TR (2010): Rethinking schizophrenia. *Nature* 468(7321): 187–93.

Insel TR (2014): The NIMH Research Domain Criteria (RDoC) Project: precision medicine for psychiatry. *Am J Psychiatry* 171(4): 395–97.

Insel TR, Gogtay N (2014): National Institute of Mental Health clinical trials: new opportunities, new expectations. *JAMA Psychiatry* 71(7): 745–46.

Jorgensen P (1998): Schizophrenic delusions: the detection of warning signals. *Schizophr Res* 22; 32(1): 17–22.

Keefe RS (2014): The longitudinal course of cognitive impairment in schizophrenia: an examination of data from premorbid through posttreatment phases of illness. *J Clin Psychiatry* 75 (Suppl 2): 8–13.

Kennedy JL et al. (2014): The social and economic burden of treatment-resistant schizophrenia: a systematic literature review. *Int Clin Psychopharmacol* 29(2): 63–76.

Kennedy WK et al. (2013): Clinically significant drug interactions with typical antipsychotics. *CNS Drugs* 27(12): 1021–48.

Keshavan MS et al. (2013) Reimagining psychoses: an agnostic approach to diagnosis. *Schizophr Res* 146(1–3): 10–16.

Keshavan MS et al. (2014): Cognitive training in mental disorders: update and future directions. *Am J Psychiatry* 171(5): 510–22.

Labrie V, Pai S, Petronis A (2012): Epigenetics of major psychosis: progress, problems and perspectives. *Trends Genet* 28(9): 427–35.

Lyman DR et al. (2014): Skill building: assessing the evidence. *Psychiatr Serv* 1;65(6): 727–38.

McGorry P et al. (2014): Biomarkers and clinical staging in psychiatry. *World Psychiatry* 13(3): 211–23.

McHugh RK et al. (2013): Patient preference for psychological vs pharmacologic treatment of psychiatric disorders: a meta-analytic review. *J Clin Psychiatry* 74(6): 595–602.

Mestdagh A, Hansen B (2014): Stigma in patients with schizophrenia receiving community mental health care: a review of qualitative studies. *Soc Psychiatry Psychiatr Epidemiol* 49(1): 79–87.

Millier A et al. (2014): Humanistic burden in schizophrenia: a literature review. *J Psychiatr Res* 54: 85–93.

Milton AC, Mullan BA (2014): Diagnosis telling in people with psychosis. *Curr Opin Psychiatry* 27(4): 302–7.

Newcomer JW et al. (2013): Switching antipsychotic medications to reduce adverse event burden in schizophrenia: establishing evidence-based practice. *J Clin Psychiatry* 74: 1108–20.

Nuechterlein KH et al. (2014): The early longitudinal course of cognitive deficits in schizophrenia. *J Clin Psychiatry* 75 (Suppl 2): 25–29.

Reddy R, Keshavan MS (2006): *Schizophrenia: A Practical Primer*. Informa, UK.

Reddy R, Yao JK, Eds (2007): *Fatty Acids and Oxidative Stress in Neuropsychiatric Disorders*. Nova Science Publishers, Hauppaugge, NY.

Reddy R, Reddy R (2011): Antioxidant therapeutics in schizophrenia. *Antioxidants & Redox Signaling* 15: 2047–2055.

Schizophrenia Working Group of the Psychiatric Genomics Consortium (2014): Biological insights from 108 schizophrenia-associated genetic loci. *Nature* 511(7510): 421–27.

Sin J, Norman I (2013): Psychoeducational interventions for family members of people with schizophrenia: a mixed-method systematic review. *J Clin Psychiatry* 74(12): e1145–62.

Tandon R, Keshavan MS, Nasrallah HA (2008): Schizophrenia, "Just the Facts": what we know in 2008 part 1: overview. *Schizophr Res* 100(1–3): 4–19.

Testart J et al. (2013): Quality of life and other outcome measures in caregivers of patients with schizophrenia. *Expert Rev Pharmacoecon Outcomes Res* 13(5): 641–49.

Thomas N et al. (2014): Psychological therapies for auditory hallucinations (voices): current status and key directions for future research. *Schizophr Bull* 40 (Suppl 4): S202–12.

Zipursky RB et al. (2014): Risk of symptom recurrence with medication discontinuation in first-episode psychosis: a systematic review. *Schizophr Res* 152(2–3): 408–14.

Index

Page numbers in *italics* indicate a figure or table on the designated page.

ABC model of cognitive behavioral therapy (CBT), 79, *79*

ABCs of coping with hallucinations, *123*

Abilify (aripiprazole), *62*, *175*

Acceptance and commitment therapy, 80

Acting-out, 165

ACT services. *See* Assertive Community Treatment (ACT) services

Adherence. *See* Treatment adherence strategies; Treatment nonadherence

Adler, Shannon L., 112

Affect, 165

Affective blunting (negative symptom), 26, 165

Affordable Care Act (ACA), 132

Agranulocytosis, 165

Akathisia, 65, 67–68, 165

Alcohol and drug abuse, 6–7, 32, 43, 44, 46, 65, 91–92, 126–27

Allele, 165

Alogia (negative symptom), 26, 165

American Psychiatric Association, 178, 179

Anhedonia (negative symptom), 26, 165

Anorgasmia, *74*, 165

Antipsychotic drugs (APDs), 5; choice factors, 61, 66; combining medications with, 64; commonly used (individual drugs), *175–76*; description, 61; duration of treatment, 63; first-generation APDs, 61, *62*, 66; liquid preparations, 62; long-acting injectables, 63; options for ineffectiveness of, 64–65; rapid-acting injections, 62; second-generation APDs, 61, *62*, 66; *start low and go slow* approach, 63; symptom relief success data, 66; tablets and capsules, 62. *See also* individual drugs

Antipsychotic drugs (APDs), side effects, 67–75, *175–76*; akathisia, 65, 67–68, 165; anorgasmia, *74*; blurred vision, 71; constipation, 71; decreased libido, *74*; diabetes, 70; dysphoria, *72*; dystonia, 68, *73–74*; early detection and management, 75; erectile dysfunction, *73*; hypercholesterolemia, 71; hyperprolactinemia, *73*; hyperthermia, *75*; leukopenia, 71; metabolic syndrome, 68–69, 75; neuroleptic malignant syndrome,

73, 75; orthostatic hypotension, 73; Parkinsonism, 68; QT-prolongation, 72; sedation, 74; seizures, 74; sialorrhea, 72; tachycardia, 73; tardive dyskinesia, 68, 75; weight gain, 69–70, 75; xerostomia, 72
Antisocial personality disorder, 32
Anxiolytics, 33, 34
APDs. *See* Antipsychotic drugs
Aripiprazole (Abilify), 62, 175
Arrests, management of, 137–39
Asenapine (Saphris), 62, 175
Asociality (negative symptom), 26, 28, 32, 46, 165
Assertive Community Treatment (ACT) services, 81–82, 105, 137, 141, 142
Assisted Outpatient Treatment (AOT), 137
Athetosis, 165
Attention, 165
Auditory hallucinations, 21–22, 22
Autism spectrum disorders, 32–33
Autoimmune disorders, 33
Automatic thoughts (in CBT), 78
Avolition (negative symptom), 26, 166

BARRED strategy for coping with delusions, 123
Bateson, Gregory, 167
A Beautiful Mind film, 11
Behavioral disturbances, 27–28
Bergson, Henri, 19
Biological foundations of schizophrenia, 145–57; environmental factors, 39–40, 149; epigenetic factors, 149; familial component, 146; identification of related-genes, 148–49; paternal age, 149; season of birth, 149; transmission, 146–47; underlying brain mechanisms, 149–57. *See also* Brain mechanisms underlying schizophrenia

Bipolar disorder, 31, 35, 92, 145
Birchwood, Max, 94
Bleuler, Eugen, 178
Blurred vision, 71
BMI (body mass index), 69, 69, 166
Borderline personality disorder, 32
Brain imaging (CT or MRI), 45
BRAIN (Brain Research through Advancing Innovative Neurotechnologies) Initiative, 159
Brain mechanisms underlying schizophrenia, 149–57; cell membrane alterations, oxidative stress pathways, 154–55, 155; dopamine (DA), 152, 152–53, 153; gamma amino butyric acid, 153; glutamate, 153–54; neuroanatomical alterations, 150–51; neurochemical alterations, 151–53; neurotransmitter systems, 154; noradrenaline, 154; onset of illness, 155–57; prefrontal cortex, 151, 170; serotonin, 154; ventricle enlargement, brain atrophy, 150
Brexpiprazole (drug under development), 162
Brief psychotic disorder, 30, 35

Cannon, Tyrone, 151
Caregiver burden, 116
Caregiver burnout: avoidance strategies, 116–19, 121; defined, 116–17, 121; reasons for developing, 117; signs and symptoms, 14, 112, 117–18, 120
Caregivers: avoiding total dependence on, 12; continuity of care considerations, 119–20, 121; defusing, de-escalation skills, 13; demands made on, 114–16; focus on healthy lifestyle, 70, 113; manual for, 112–21; medication management, 113; multiple roles of, 85, 112–14; necessity of self-care, 118–19; need for planning for the future, 16;

symptom identification and management, 113–14; use of rewards by, 87

CARE LIST mnemonic (psycho-education principles), 77, 78

Care team: assembling the team, 47, 104–11; caregiver communication with, 113; case managers, 81, 82, 105–6; counselors and psychologists, 106; difficulties in maintaining, 103; getting referrals from, 8; giving consent to, 59; making changes to, 109–10, 111; medication management, 5–6, 70, 73–74, 75, 85, 86; patient advocacy role, 12; peer counselors, 107, 111; primary care physicians, 105; psychiatric nurses, 106, 111; psychiatrists, 5, 61, 105–11; questions to ask about treatment providers, 108–9; reaching out to, 7, 9, 13, 14, 74; role of insurance plan, 107–8; screening for substance abuse, 92–93; side effect management, 73; social workers, 105, 111; strategies for working with, 15, 52; and treatment nonadherence, 83–84, 91; treatment plan creation, management, 26, 33, 58–61, 64–65, 68, 70, 75, 76, 80, 94; treatment-specific therapists, 106

Cariprazine (drug under development), 162

Case management: description, 81, 82; intermittent supervision by, 129; as member of care team, 111; methods of locating, 105–6; referrals to treatment-specific therapists, 106; as rehabilitation component, 81

Case Management Society of America, 81

Catatonia, 166

Catatonic excitement, 28

Catatonic stupor, 28

CATIE (Clinical Antipsychotic Trials of Intervention Effectiveness) trial, 166

CBT. *See* Cognitive behavioral therapy (CBT)

Cerebrovascular disorders, 33

Chlorpromazine (Thorazine, Largactil), 62, 175

Chorea, 166

Cigarette smoking, 70, 93, 96

Circumstantiality (disordered thinking), 23, 166

Clinical history, 44–45

Clinical worsening of symptoms: causes of, 134, 140; decompensation phase, 134–5, 166; relapse phase, 135, 171

Clozapine (Clozaril), 59, 62, 92, 175

Clozaril (clozapine), 59, 62, 92, 175

Cocaine: causative for psychosis, 152; possible link to schizophrenia, 33, 34, 44, 92

Coexisting with schizophrenia: allowing room for emotions, 99; avoiding blame, 99, 100; care team maintenance, 101–2, 103; initial reaction to diagnosis, 99–100; making peace with taking medications, 102; recognizing sources of stress, 101; staying positive, 101; telling other about diagnosis, 101; utilizing psychotherapy modalities, 102

Cognition, 166

Cognitive abnormalities, 28

Cognitive Adaptation Training, 79

Cognitive behavioral therapy (CBT), 77–79, 82; ABC model of, 79, 79; assessment and engagement phase, 79; associated terminology, 78; behavior change phase, 79; consolidation phase, 79

Cognitive enhancement therapy (CET), 79–80

Cognitive remediation therapies, 9

Cognitive restructuring (in CBT), 78

Collaborations in treatment, 15, 58–59, 66, 81. *See also* Therapeutic alliances

Communicating with schizophrenics, 11–12

Complete blood count (CBC), 45

Compliance therapy, 87–88

Consta (risperidone), *62*, 175

Constipation, *71*

Coping skills, 7

Core features of schizophrenia. *See* Symptoms of schizophrenia

Course and prognosis of schizophrenia, 49–53

Crawford, Roger, 99

Crisis management, 13–14, 134–42; ACT, AOT services, 81–82, 105–6, 137, 141, 142; adverse life events, 140; consideration of hospitalization, 136–37; crisis resource identification, 141–42; defusing crises process, 135; expressed emotion (EE), 140–41; nonadherence treatment, 139, *139*; physical illnesses, 140; prevention strategies, 139–41; recognizing crises, 136; side effects of medications, 140; substance abuse, 140; working with law enforcement, 137–39

CT (computed tomography), 45, 150, 166

Cuthbert, Bruce, 160, 179

CUtLASS (Cost Utility of the Latest Antipsychotic drugs in Schizophrenia Study), 166

Cytochrome P450, 166

Cytogenetic/congenital disorders, *33*

Decompensation, 134–5, 166

Decreased libido, *74*

Defiance (Redwine), 134

Defusing crises, 135

Delirium, 166

Delusional disorder, 31

Delusions: and aggressive behavior, 13; BARRED strategy for coping with, *123*; in bipolar disorder, 31; in borderline personality disorder, 32; categories of, 20, *21*; CBT for, 78, 82; comparison of hallucinations, 21; defined, 4, 19, 20, 166; MCT for, 80, 82; in mood disorders, 31; portrayal in *A Beautiful Mind,* 11; as a positive symptom, 19, 28; in schizoaffective disorder, 30; as a type of psychosis, 29

Delusions of passivity, *21*, 46

Dementia, 159, 166

Dendrites, 166

Denial, 85, 99, 166

Depression: as bipolar disorder component, 31; and caregiver burnout, 14; impact on recovery, 91–92; postpsychotic depression, 91; as prodromal symptom, 43, 92; in schizoaffective disorder, 30; as schizophrenia symptom, 27; use of CBT for, 77

Derailment, 46, 167, 169

Developmental model of schizophrenia, *156*

Diabetes, 5, 68, 70, 75, 83, 140

Diagnosis of schizophrenia: age of onset, 41; clinical history, 44–45; commonly observed prodromal symptoms, 43; core symptom identification, 19; DSM-5 criteria, 46; early diagnosis, 42, 58; getting a second opinion, 47–48; ICD-10 criteria, 46–47; identification challenges, 10, 29, 42; learning to live with, 99–100; medical testing, 45–46; mental status examination, 45, 48; onset of process, 43; psychiatric evaluation, 10, 44, 45, 48, 137–8; related fears, 3; ruling out non-schizophrenic disorders, 29, 35; telling others about, 101

Diagnostic and Statistical Manual of Mental Disorders, Fifth Edition (DSM-V), 46, 48, 160
Dietary disorders, *33*
Differential diagnosis of schizophrenia (TACTICS MDS USE), *33*
Disordered thinking, 4, 167; circumstantiality, *23*; cognitive remediation therapies for, 9; and compromised communication, 11, *23*; disorder patterns, *25*; flight of ideas, *23*; loose associations, *23*; neologism, *23*; perseveration, *23*; symptoms, *23*; tangentiality, *23*; thought blocking, *23*; types of, *24*
Dissociative identity disorder (multiple personality disorder), 32, 35
Dopamine excess theory, *152*
Dopamine hypothesis revision, *153*
Double-bind theory, 167
Double-blind design, 167
Downward drift hypothesis, 167
Drug abuse. *See* Alcohol and drug abuse
Dyskinesia, 167
Dysphoria, *72*, 167
Dystonia, 68, *73–74*, 167

Eack, Shaun, 80
Early diagnosis, 42, *58*
Early Signs Scale (Birchwood), 94
Echolalia, 27–28, 167
Echopraxia, 27, 167
Effectiveness (of treatment), 167
Efficacy, 167
Electroconvulsive therapy (ECT), 64
Emotion, 167
Emotional (affective) disturbances, 4, 27
Empathy, 167
Empirical, 167
Employment issues, 130–31
Encenicline (drug under development), *162*
Endocrine disorders, *33*

Endophenotype, 167
Epigenetics, 149
EPS (extrapyramidal symptoms), 167
Erectile dysfunction, *73*
Erotomania, 168
Esquirol, Dominique, 178
Ethnicity, 168
Executive functions, 79, 168
Exercise, 14, *71*, *78*, 124
Expressed emotions, 10, 168

Faith, 168
Families of schizophrenics: genetic component of schizophrenia, 8; high expressed emotions in, 10; impact on treatment, 12; questions asked by, 9–16; risk factors for "catching" schizophrenia, 11; setting rules and expectations, 14–15
Fanapt (iloperidone), 62, *175*
First-episode psychosis, 63
First-generation APDs, 61, *62*
Flat affect, 46, 118, 168
Flight of ideas, *24*, *25*, 168
Fluphenazine (Prolixin, Permitil), 62, 68, *176*
fMRI (functional magnetic resonance imaging), 168
Food stamps, 128, 133
Franzen, Goran, 178
Freud, Sigmund, 178
Friends of schizophrenics: impact on treatment, 12; questions asked by, 9–16; risk factors for "catching" schizophrenia, 11; setting rules and expectations, 14–15
Future treatment directions, 158–63; development of better treatments, 161–63; induced pluripotent stem cells, 159; neurobiology of psychoses research, 159; optogenetics, 159; pharmacological research and trials, 161–63, *162*; psychosis prevention, 159, *161*, 163

Gender, 168
Gene, 168
Genetic component of schizophrenia, 8
Geodon (ziprasidone), 62, *175*
Girl in Translation (Kwok), 36
Gliosis, 168
Goal of schizophrenia treatment, 5
Grandiose, 168
Gustatory, 168
Gustatory (taste) hallucinations, *23*

Haldol (haloperidol), 62, 68, *176*
Hallucinations, 4, 10; ABCs of
coping with, *123*; auditory, 21–22,
22; and communication difficulties,
11; delusional thinking compar-
ison, 21; description, 4, 20–21,
168; gustatory, *23*; olfactory, *23*;
portrayal in *A Beautiful Mind,* 11;
somatosensory, *23*; visual, *22*
Hallucinogens, *33, 34,* 169. *See also*
LSD (lysergic acid diethylamide)
Haloperidol (Haldol), 62, 176
Health system challenges, 131–32
Hearing voices, 4, 20, *22,* 34, 35,
123, 136
Hecker, Ewald, 178
Heritability of schizophrenia, 146,
149, 157, 168
Hogarty, Gerard, 80
Housing issues, 129–30, 133
Human Brain Project, 159
Human Connectome Project, 159
Hypercholesterolemia, *71*
Hyperprolactinemia, *73,* 168
Hyperthermia, *75*
Hypnotics, *33, 34,* 65
Hypochondriacal, 168

Iatrogenic disorders, *33*
Ideas of reference, 168
Illusion, 168
Iloperidone (Fanapt), 62, *175*
Inappropriate affect, 27, 168

Incidence, 168
Incidence of newly diagnosed schizo-
phrenia, 37
Induced pluripotent stem cells, 159
Information-processing bias, 78
Informed consent by patients, 59
Ingyar, David, 178
Inhalants, possible link to schizo-
phrenia, 34
Insel, Thomas, 160, 179
Insight, 168
Intensive case management
(ICM), 81
*International Classification of
Diseases, Tenth Edition (ICD-10),*
46, 48
Invega (paliperidone), 62
IT-007 (drug under development),
162

Jean-Étienne, 178
Jeste, Dilip, 179
Job skills training, 131
John Paul II (Pope), 158
Johnstone, Eve, 178
Jorgenson, P., *94*

Kahlbaum, Karl, 178
Keshavan, Matcheri, 80
Ketamine, *33,* 34
Kidney and liver function tests, 45
Kraepelin, Emil, 159, 178
Kwok, Jean, 36

Labile/lability, 169
Laing, R.D., 9
Lake, Nick, 89
Langfeldt, Gabriel, 178
Largactil (chlorpromazine), 62, *175*
Lasègue, Charles, 178
Latuda (lurasidone), 62, *175*
Law enforcement, working with,
137–39
Leukopenia, *71,* 169

Lifetime prevalence for schizophrenia, 37, 169
Lobotomy, 169
Long-acting injectable APDs, 63
Loose associations (disordered thinking), 23, 169
Loxitane (loxapine), 62, 176
LSD (lysergic acid diethylamide), 10, 34, 169
Lurasidone (Latuda), 62, 175

Magical thinking, 169
Manic-depressive disorder. See Bipolar disorder
Mannerisms, 27, 169
Marijuana: and clinical history, 44; possible link to schizophrenia, 6, 10, 34; and substance abuse, 92, 140
McGorry, Patrick, 160, 179
Medical testing, 45–46
Medication treatment: clinical drug trials, 64–65, 159, 162; combining medications, 64; determination of duration of initial trial, 60; exploration of alternative medications, 64; reasons for wanting to stop, 6–7. See also Antipsychotic drugs
Mental status examination, 45, 48
Metabolic disorders, 33
Metabolic syndrome, 68–69
Metacognition, 80
Metacognitive therapy (MCT), 80
Meyer, Adolf, 178
Mindfulness-based therapies, 80
Money and finance problems, 127
Mood disorders, 31
Morel, Benedict, 178
MRI (magnetic resonance imaging), 45, 168, 169
Muddled thinking, 4
Multifactorial, 169
Multiple personality disorder (dissociative identity disorder), 32, 35

NAMI (National Alliance on Mental Illness): clinician recommendations, 47; help with disappearance issues, 138; insurance information, 111; Planned Lifetime Assistance Network, 16; reviews of local mental health professionals, 108; sponsorship of family support groups, 9
Nash, John, 11
National Institute of Mental Health (NIMH), 159, 160
Navane (thiothixene), 62, 176
Negative symptoms of schizophrenia, 25, 26, 169; affective blunting, 26; alogia, 26; anhedonia, 26; asociality, 26, 28, 32, 46; avolition, 26; and diagnosis, 52; primary, 25; secondary, 25
Neologism (disordered thinking), 23, 169
Neurochemical alterations, 151–57; cell membrane alterations, oxidative stress, 154–55, 155; dopamine (DA), 152–53; gamma amino butyric acid, 153; glutamate, 153–54; other neurotransmitter systems, 154
Neuroleptic, 169
Neuroleptic-induced Parkinsonism, 92
Neuroleptic malignant syndrome, 73
Neurological abnormalities, 28
Neuropil, 169
Neutropenia, 169
Nonadherence to treatment. See Treatment nonadherence
NW-3509 (drug under development), 162

Obama, Barack, 159
Olanzapine (Zyprexa), 62, 68, 175
Olfaction, 169

Olfactory (smell) hallucinations, 23

Opioids, possible link to schizophrenia, 33, 34

Optogenetics, 159

Orthostatic hypotension, 73, 169

Overvalued idea, 169

Oxidative stress pathways, 154–55, 155

Paliperidone (Invega), 62

Paranoia, 169

Paranoid personality disorder, 32

Paraphrenia, 169

Parkinsonism, 68, 169

PCP (phencyclidine), hallucinogenic drug, 10, 34, 170

Peer counselors, 107, 111

Perception, 170

Perinatal complications, risk factor, 39–40, 149, 170

Permitil (fluphenazine), 62, 176

Perphenazine (Trilafon), 62, 176

Perseveration (disordered thinking), 23, 170

PET (positron emission tomography), 170

Phases of schizophrenia, 57–58

Pimozide, 176

Pinel, Phillipe, 178

Planned Lifetime Assistance Network (NAMI PLAN), 16

Plato, 30

Point prevalence, 170

Polygenic, 170

Polymorphism, 170

PORT (Schizophrenic Patient Outcome Research Team), 170

Positive symptoms of schizophrenia, 19–25, 170. *See also* Disordered thinking; Hallucinations

Postpsychotic depression, 91

Posturing, 27, 170

Poverty of content of speech, 170

Poverty of speech, 170

PREDICT outcome factors, 51–52

Prefrontal cortex, 151, 170

Premorbid, 170

Prescription drug abuse, possible link to schizophrenia, 34

Prevalence, 170

Prevalence of schizophrenia in the U.S., 37

Problems in facing schizophrenia, 122–33; ABCs of coping with hallucinations, 123; alcohol and drug abuse, 6–7, 32, 44, 65, 91–92, 126–27; behavioral issues, 124–25; employment, 130–31; food stamps, 128; health system challenges, 131–32; housing issues, 129–30; management of chronic symptoms, 123; money and finances, 127; personal and social coping skills, 125–26; public assistance, 128; SSI and SSDI, 127–28; structural issues, 127–30; VA benefits, 128–29

Prodromal symptoms, 43, 46, 57–58, 66, 153, 162, 165

Prognosis, 170

Prognostication of schizophrenia, 50–52; defined, 50–51; favorable *vs.* unfavorable factors, 53; PREDICT outcome factors, 51–52

Progressive model of schizophrenia, 156

Prolixin (fluphenazine), 62, 176

Psychiatric evaluation, 10, 44, 45, 48, 137, 138

Psychiatric nurses, 106, 111

Psychoeducation, 77, 78, 82, 170

Psychological treatments: acceptance and commitment therapy, 80; Cognitive Adaptation Training, 79; cognitive behavioral therapy, 77–79, 82; cognitive enhancement therapy, 79–80; metacognition, 80; metacognitive therapy, 80;

mindfulness-based therapies, 80; psychoeducation, 77, 78, 82; social skills training, 80–81, 82; supportive psychotherapy, 5, 77

Psychosis: associated disorders, 30–33; culturally sanctioned psychotic behavior, 34–35; defined, 29–30, 170; first-episode psychosis, 63; future treatment directions, 159, 161, 163; and insomnia, 65; medication treatment, 64; and obtaining consent for treatment, 59

Psychotic episodes: agitation during, 65; consequence of delayed treatment, 91; and depression, 92; insomnia during, 65; and prodromal symptoms, 58; studies of gray brain matter volume reductions, 153

Public assistance programs, 128, 133

QTc interval, 170
QT-prolongation, 72
Questions asked by family and friends, 9–16
Quetiapine (Seroquel), 62, 175

Race, 170
Recovery, 171
Recovery maximization, 89–96; and cigarette smoking, 93, 96; conditions complication recovery, 91–93; Early Signs Scale, 94; individualization of treatment, 95; influential factors, 90–91; maintaining the right attitude, 95; relapse prevention, 93–95; and smoking, 93; and substance abuse, 91, 92–93, 95; Warning Signal Scale, 94

Redwine, C. J., 134
Rehabilitative treatments: assertive community treatment, 81–82; case management, 81, 82; intensive case management, 81

Relapse, 171
Relapse prevention, 93–95
Relaxation techniques (in CBT), 78
Research Domain Criteria (R-DoC), 159
Restricted affect, 171
Risk factors for schizophrenia: age, 37; ethnicity, race, geographic location, 39; family history, 38–39; immigration status, 39, 41; paternal age, 40; perinatal complications, 39–40, 149; season of birth, 40; sex (gender), 38; urban area birth, 40, 149. See also Biological foundations of schizophrenia

Risperidone (Risperdal, Consta), 62, 175
Routines, planning and sticking to, 124
RP5063 (drug under development), 162

Safe sex, 7
Saphris (asenapine), 62, 175
SARDAA (Schizophrenia and Related Disorders Alliance of America), 9
Schizoaffective disorder, 30, 35
Schizoid personality disorder, 31, 35
Schizophrenia: associated definitions, 37; biological foundations of, 145–57; clinical worsening of, 134–35, 140, 166, 171; coexisting with, 99–142; common problems in facing, 122–33; contributors to research directions, 178–79; course and prognosis of, 49–53; developmental, progressive models of, 156; differential diagnosis of, 33; four phases of, 57–58; historical background, 177–79; medical treatment, 57–66; prognostication of, 50–52, 51–52, 53; psychological, rehabilitative treatments, 76–82;

strategies for coexisting with, 99–103; term origin, 28; waxing and waning of symptoms, 13. *See also* Symptoms of schizophrenia

Schizophrenia Working Group, 179

Schizophreniform disorder, 30, 35

Schizotypal personality disorder, 31

Schneider, Kurt, 178

Second-generation APDs, 61, 62

Second opinion evaluation, 47–48

Sedatives, possible link to schizophrenia, 33, 34

Seizure disorders, 33

Selective serotonin reuptake inhibitors (SSRIs), 92

Self-efficacy, 171

Sepsis/infective disorders, 33

Seroquel (quetiapine), 62, 175

Sheltered employment, 131

Sialorrhea, 72, 171

Side effects of antipsychotic drugs (APDs). *See* Antipsychotic drugs (APDs), side effects

Single-blind design, 171

Sleep-deprived EEG testing, 45

Smoking. *See* Cigarette smoking

Social Security Disability Insurance (SSDI), 127–28, 133

Social skills training (SST), 5, 80–82, 125–26

Social workers, 105, 111

Somatic, 171

Somatosensory, 171

Somatosensory (physical sensations and balance) hallucinations, 23

Space-occupying disorders, 33

Stelazine (trifluoperazine), 62, 176

Stereotypes, 27, 171

Stigma, 171

Strayed, Cheryl, 89

Street drugs: need for avoidance, 7; possible links to schizophrenia, 10, 34. *See also* Alcohol and drug abuse

Stress management and reduction, 124, 125

Stupor, 28, 74, 166, 171

Substance abuse. *See* Alcohol and drug abuse

Suicidal ideation, 31

Supplemental needs trusts, 120

Supplemental Security Income (SSI), 127–28, 133

Supported employment, 131

Supportive psychotherapy (ST), 5, 77

Symptoms of schizophrenia: behavioral disturbances, 27–28; clinical worsening of, 134–35, 140, 166, 171; cognitive abnormalities, 28; delusions, 13, 19–20, 21; emotional disturbances, 4, 27; hearing voices, 4, 20, 22, 34, 35, 123, 136; inappropriate affect, 27; life management choices, 8; male *vs.* female onset, 41; need for avoiding street drugs, 10; negative symptoms, 25–26; neurological abnormalities, 28; paranoia, 13; positive symptoms, 19–23; prodromal, 43, 46, 57–58, 65, 153, 162, 165; waxing and waning of, 13. *See also* Disordered thinking; Hallucinations

Syndrome, 171

Tachycardia, 73

TACTICS MDS USE mnemonic, 33

Tangentiality (disordered thinking), 23, 171

Tardive dyskinesia, 68, 167, 171

Temporary Assistance to Needy Families (TANF) programs, 128

THC (tetrahydrocannabinol), 171. *See also* Marijuana

Therapeutic alliances, 58, 66, 110, 171. *See also* Collaborations in treatment

Thiothixene (Navane), 62, 176

Thorazine (chlorpromazine), 62, 176

Thought blocking (disordered thinking), *23*, 171
Thought broadcasting, *21*, 46, 171
Thought insertion, *21*, 46, 171
Thyroid function testing, 45
Titration, 171
Toxic/substance-induced disorders, *33*
Transitional employment, 131
Transmission of schizophrenia, 146–47
Treatment adherence strategies: communication with care team, 86; compliance therapy, 87–88; injectable, long-acting APDs, 87, 88; keep prescriptions filled, 87; medication-related routines, 87; monitor recovery, 87; pill boxes, 88; side effects management, 86; use rewards, 87; written schedules, 88
Treatment nonadherence, 83–88; complex treatment schedules, 85; defined, 88; excessive costs of treatments, 85–86; ineffectiveness of medications, 85; lack of awareness of one's illness, 84–85; reasons for, 83–84, *84*, 88; stigma related to treatment, 86; undesirable side effects, 84
Treatment of schizophrenia: associated modalities, 7, 8; collaborations, 15, 58–59, 66, 81; crisis management, 13–14; duration of, 6; early diagnosis, interventions, 58; general principles, 57–59; goal of, 5; having a "Plan B," 60; identification of key symptoms, 59–60; impact of family and friends, 12; monitoring of side effects, 60; monitoring patient compliance, 60; patient consent, 59; therapeutic alliances, 58, 66, 110, 171; things to avoid, 7. *See also* Antipsychotic drugs; Future treatment directions; Medication treatment; Psychological treatments
Trifluoperazine (Stelazine), 62, *176*
Trilafon (perphenazine), 62, *176*

Urine drug/toxicology screen, 45

Veterans Administration (VA) benefits, 128–29, 133
Violent behavior, risk factors, 12–13
Voices. *See* Hearing voices

Warning Signal Scale (WSS), 94, *94*
Watson, James D., 145
Weight gain, 69–70
Weinberger, Daniel, 179
Winter, Sarah, 122
Word salad, 171
Wright, Nicola, 80

Xerostomia, 72

Ziprasidone (Geodon), 62, *175*
Zyprexa (olanzapine), 62, 68, *175*

About the Authors

RAVINDER REDDY, MD, is adjunct professor of psychiatry at the University of Pittsburgh School of Medicine and specializes in the treatment, research, and particularly the teaching of schizophrenia. He received specialized training at the University of New Mexico and New York State Psychiatric Institute/Columbia University. He was the psychiatry residency training director at the University of Pittsburgh for many years, and trained over a hundred psychiatrists. He has over 25 years of clinical experience with schizophrenia, in inpatient and outpatient settings, as well as working with the homeless. He has been funded by the National Institute of Mental Health and NARASD (research branch of National Alliance for the Mentally Ill) to conduct research into schizophrenia. He is the recipient of the Pittsburgh Schizophrenia Conference Award. He has previously published 2 books, *Schizophrenia: A Practical Primer* and *Fatty Acids and Oxidative Stress in Neuropsychiatric Disorders*, and 10 book chapters on various topics in schizophrenia. He has been a reviewer for over 20 professional journals.

MATCHERI S. KESHAVAN, MD, is Stanley Cobb Professor, vice-chair for Public Psychiatry at the Beth Israel Deaconess Medical Center and the Massachusetts Mental Health Center, Harvard Medical School. He completed his psychiatric training at the National Institute of Mental Health and Neurosciences (NIMHANS) in Bangalore (India), Vienna, London, and Detroit. Dr. Keshavan is closely involved in research into neurobiology and early interventions in psychotic disorders. His research has resulted in over 500 publications, including over 350 peer-reviewed papers, 4 books, and 20 book chapters. He has received several awards, including the Gaskell Gold Medal of the Royal College of Psychiatrists (1985), the Research Scientist Development Award from NIMH, and the 2003 NAMI (National Alliance for the Mentally Ill of Pennsylvania) Psychiatrist of the Year Award. He is a distinguished Fellow of the American Psychiatric Association, a Fellow of the Royal College of Physicians, Canada, and a Fellow of the Royal College of Psychiatrists, United Kingdom. Dr. Keshavan is the editor in chief of the *Asian Journal of Psychiatry* (Elsevier) and serves on the editorial board for journals such as the *Acta Neuropsychiatrica*, *Clinical Schizophrenia*, *Bipolar Disorders*, and *Schizophrenia Research*.